The House of a Million Pets

ANN HODGMAN

The House of a Million Pets

with illustrations by
Eugene Yelchin

Henry Holt and Company
New York

*To the Sunday School at St. John's Church,
Washington, Connecticut—and to Banjie*

Henry Holt and Company, LLC
Publishers since 1866
175 Fifth Avenue
New York, New York 10010
www.HenryHoltKids.com

Henry Holt® is a registered trademark of Henry Holt and Company, LLC.
Text copyright © 2007 by Ann Hodgman
Illustrations copyright © 2007 by Eugene Yelchin
All rights reserved.
Distributed in Canada by H. B. Fenn and Company Ltd.

Library of Congress Cataloging-in-Publication Data
Hodgman, Ann.
The house of a million pets / Ann Hodgman.—1st ed.
p.   cm.
ISBN-13: 978-0-8050-7974-6
ISBN-10: 0-8050-7974-2
1. Hodgman, Ann—Juvenile literature.   2. Pet owners—Connecticut—
Washington—Biography—Juvenile literature.   3. Pets—Connecticut—
Washington—Anecdotes—Juvenile literature.   I. Title.
SF411.45.H63A3 2007   636.088'7092—dc22   [B]   2006036447

First Edition—2007 / Designed by Amy Manzo Toth
Printed in the United States of America on acid-free paper. ∞

1 3 5 7 9 10 8 6 4 2

*A portion of the profits from the sale of this book will be donated
to the Humane Society of the United States.*

Each species experiences the world differently, and many species have capacities that are far different from ours. They can show us the *unimaginable*. Thus, the greater our empathy with a variety of animals, the more we can learn.

—*Bernd Heinrich,* Winter World

introduction

Here's how old I am: FIFTY-ONE.

I bet you think that's horribly old.

Here's what I look like. —

I bet *you* wouldn't want to look like that.

I bet you think you have more fun than I do, because you're a kid and you get to play and I'm an old hag who just sits around mourning the past.

You are so, so wrong.

Being old is *way* better than being young— because when you're a grownup, no one can keep you from doing what you want. If you want to play music as loud as possible, go ahead! Your mom doesn't live with you anymore. She can't scream, "Turn it down!"

If you want to buy a huge bag of candy bars and eat it all yourself, go ahead! No one's going to warn you about cavities or say Americans eat too much junk food. And if your teeth all fall out, you can just buy some more teeth!

If! you! want! to! write! a! paragraph! with! lots! of! exclamation! points! do! it!!! No teacher is looking over your shoulder. When you're a grownup, you don't get grades.

We're talking about near-total freedom here. "Near" because if you're a grownup, you might have a few responsibilities. You know—jobs, and kids you have to take care of, and so on. But I think you would agree that that's not much of a problem. Because kids *prefer* parents who buy big bags of candy and turn the music up to maximum volume (as long as the parents don't dance in front of the kids' friends and humiliate them).

Kids also like parents who buy lots and lots of pets.

Now, speaking as an adult, I have to say that many parents are not so great in this area. For some reason, they don't like the idea of adding animals to the household. There's a lot of "You can't have that hamster because *I'll* end up taking care of it." Or "We don't need a dog. This house is crazy enough already." Or "You know Grandpa is allergic to cats."

Well, I'm not that kind of grownup.

When I was your age, or maybe a little younger, all I wanted was more and more animals. I always had a dog, of course, and a hamster or two, and maybe a guinea pig. Once, for a very short time, we had a parakeet. One day, my dog calmly picked it up in her jaws and began to carry it away. We rescued the bird. (Well, my younger sister did—I ran screaming out of the room.) But somehow it never seemed like quite enough. When I grew up, I realized, now's my chance. And I began to track down all the pets I'd never had.

Hedgehogs. Dogs. Prairie dogs. Cats. A baby owl. Baby robins, blue jays, and starlings. Dozens of canaries. A few parakeets. Regular mice. Baby wild mice whom I fed from an eyedropper. A family of African pygmy mice no bigger than a quarter. A family of seven rats who lived in a big cage on my kitchen table. Several turtles who lived in my bathtub. Ducklings who lived in a wading pool on my porch. A baby bat. A vole. Sugar gliders. (They're like flying squirrels, only they have a pouch like a kangaroo.) Rabbits. A cockatiel named Japan. A bulbul. (Look it up.) Baby snapping turtles the size of a bottle cap. An albino frog. Tadpoles, of course. And, yes, hamsters. Why would I say to my kids, "You can't have that hamster because I'll end up taking care of it"? I *want* to take care of hamsters!

And those are some—just some!—of the animals who have lived with my family and me over the past few years. There are more. For instance, I also raise moths. All summer I take care of the caterpillars—luna and cecropia caterpillars, who grow as big as a man's thumb. I keep their cocoons on the porch all winter long. The next spring they hatch into huge, beautiful moths and fly away into the night.

I don't mind that I'm the one who ended up taking care of all the pets. It would be ridiculous for me to mind, when I'm the one who bought them.

I don't mind that the animals make the house kind of a mess, what with the hay and the floating fur and the feathers and the rabbit droppings on the floor. It's my house, and my pets can do whatever they want to it.

Whenever kids hear about my animals, they ask me why I've never written a book about them.

So finally I decided to do it. And here it is.

the barnyard

Welcome to my barnyard.

Actually, it's my basement. It only *looks* like a barnyard—a barnyard inside a house. The half of the basement that's clean belongs to my husband, David,

and my kids, Laura and John. The half that's covered with hay and poop and seeds and shredded newspaper and feathers and bits of lettuce and spiderwebs belongs to me—or, rather, to the smaller pets who live with us.

"It kind of smells down here," a four-year-old visitor once told me. And that's true. You can't have a barnyard in your house without a *little* bit of smell. Besides, take a whiff of a real barnyard and you'll see that mine is a beautiful, perfumed garden by comparison.

Of course the "clean" half of the basement is really only clean-ish. You can't have dozens of animals in one spot without a *little* bit of mess spreading out to the rest of the area. And I'm working on a dollhouse miniature general store, which I cannot possibly do where all the pets are. (I can't have fur getting all over my miniature supplies, can I?) So the store is set up in my family's half of the basement as well.

When you think about it, David and Laura and John don't really get their full share of the basement. So I try never to think about it.

That screaming you hear? It's coming from my bulbul, Quaker. She thinks of her tuneless noise as singing. I don't complain, because when Quaker first came to live here she was too sad to make a sound. I like knowing that she's happy enough to screech a little. I just wish I could figure out a way to help her keep her feathers from falling out.

Here's my cage of little birds—Gouldian finches and canaries. Don't they look like flowers? Well, flowers with wings and beaks? What I'm trying to say is, aren't they beautiful? They don't have a lot of personality (especially compared with Quaker), but they make up for it by being so colorful.

The whistling squeaks you hear are coming from my three guinea pigs: Rein, Plumpy, and Frowny. They want some greens, and they want them *right now.* They've forgotten that I gave them a pile of spinach twenty minutes ago—either that, or they know that every time they squeal for food there's a good chance of getting some.

Meanwhile, my big gray rabbit Stumper has realized that the guinea pigs are about to be fed, so he's coming over for a treat as well. Stumper runs in a lolloping, lopsided way; he has only three legs. Poor Stumps is lonely these days. His companion rabbit, Blink, died a few months ago.

Now, Maisie, the last of my prairie dogs, is starting to rustle around and chirp as well. Maisie doesn't care much about food; what she wants is to be patted. I scoop her out of her cage and tuck her into her Snugli. That way I can carry her around while I take care of the rest of the animals.

The two little rabbits, Mojo and Crosby, know I'm about to let them out of their pen for some "floor time." To them, floor time means a chance to check under the birdcages for any stray birdseed. It also means a chance to plant themselves at the edge of their fence and stare coldly at Stumper. (Stumper and Mojo are mortal enemies, at least from tiny Mojo's point of view.) Mojo is waiting eagerly at the door of the pen. I give him a scratch on the nose. I reach over and try to pat Crosby, but she only growls at me. Have you ever heard a rabbit growl? Crosby does it whenever I touch her. She's really Mojo's rabbit, not mine.

The hamster and the twenty-six pygmy mice are still sleeping in the deep burrows they've made in their cages. They won't stir until I turn the basement lights off at night. Once in a while the hamster staggers up for a little fresh air during the day, like a miniature groundhog on February 2. But I hardly ever see the pygmy mice. Still, I like knowing they're there.

Have you noticed that most of my animals have the same shape—long and low to the ground? My two dachshunds look like that, too. Right now they're hovering at the top of the basement stairs, wishing they had the nerve to come down and see what's going on. And my three cats—the only long-legged creatures I own—are staring in through the basement windows. They're probably thinking, "Look! There's some prey! Prey that she's fattening up for *us*!" They're never allowed in the basement—in fact, they're never allowed into my house (they have their own)—but they never give up hope.

One way or another, I spend quite a lot of time down here. I hope you'll like my barnyard as much as I do.

meet the dogs

It hardly counts to include my dogs as pets. Dogs are members of the family, don't you think? But since it would hurt my dogs' feelings not to be mentioned first, I'll introduce them here.

They're named Moxie and Beanie. Moxie is the black and tan one. She's twelve years old. Beanie is the

brown one, and he's six. Beanie is the one with the worst breath on the planet. Moxie is the one with the worst breath in the universe. No matter how often we have her soft greenish brown teeth cleaned, her breath smells like thousands of dead lobsters. She also barks every minute, all day long, when she isn't sleeping. She goes especially nuts when she hears someone knock at the door. In fact, you can knock on the wall right next to her head and she'll start barking. And she pees a little bit every time someone outside our family pats her.

Actually, Moxie's kind of a dud. When the kids and I met with a dachshund breeder who had a litter of puppies for sale, we picked out an adorable seven-week-old female puppy whom all three of us loved right away. David came with us when we drove to get her the next week. To our surprise, he didn't like the puppy we'd picked out. He thought she was too jumpy and squeaky.

"I like this one better," he said, pointing to Moxie, who was sitting there staring at the air. "She seems calmer."

The breeder frowned. "That puppy doesn't have much on the ball," she said.

When a *breeder* tells you one of her dogs isn't that great, you should listen!

"I still think we should take her." David turned to us. "Would that be okay?"

The kids and I weren't ecstatic about the change, but we said okay. All the puppies were darling. It wasn't as if David was suggesting that we replace our first-choice pup with a spider. But the breeder was very grouchy about it.

"Three people came this week who wanted the *first* puppy you chose," she said. "I had to turn them down."

"Well, now you'll be able to tell them yes!" I said. And we drove home with Moxie.

David now says, "Moxie *was* quieter than the other female. What if we'd taken the other female and she had been even noisier than this?" Anyway, we all love Moxie, despite her dud-ness. But every now and then, when she's being especially crazy, I'll mutter, "You weren't our first choice, you know."

Then I give her a kiss on her smelly, smelly muzzle, because what if she'd gone home with some other family who didn't appreciate her for what she was? A family who actually got mad at her barking and jumping and peeing on the floor? That would have been terrible. No, I guess Moxie's in the right place.

You will notice that Moxie and Beanie are both miniature dachshunds, or what idiots call "hot dog dogs." "Look at the little hot dogs," people always say when I'm taking Moxie and Beanie on a walk. I want to ask, "Do you think you're the first person who's ever said that?" But I never get the chance, because the second anyone tries to talk to us, Moxie starts barking. If the person who stops to talk is walking a dog, Beanie begins screaming like a teakettle. He really does *shriek* whenever he sees another dog; he's a total coward. He's also scared if we drive to the woods and take a walk, because he doesn't like to leave the car behind. During the whole time, he'll be checking over his shoulder to make sure the car is still there. He's really only happy when I turn around and we head back toward the car. I wish I could park the car and have a helicopter waiting to drop me and the dogs far enough away from the car that Beanie would stop fretting during our walks.

SO WHAT *CAN* THEY DO?

I guess it's obvious that Moxie and Beanie aren't much good at the things *real* dogs do, like rescuing people in the Alps or jumping over Niagara Falls to find the park ranger. They're certainly nothing like my sister and brother-in-law's Australian shepherds, Rory and Scout. Once, my brother-in-law was taking Rory along to gather duck eggs at his farm when he realized that something was wrong with a dam in a nearby brook. He put down the empty basket and went to check the dam. When he returned, the basket contained an egg, and Rory was coming back from the duck house with another egg in her mouth. She had figured out how to gather the eggs all by herself.

Here's what *my* dogs are good at: snuggling. As anyone who owns a miniature dachshund knows, you cannot sleep at night unless the dog is in bed with you. Oh, you might sleep *better* without the dog. Dachshunds sometimes like to stand on your back and do a little digging into your skin for no reason. And if they get too hot under the covers, they like to put their head on the pillow right next to yours and breathe their dead-lobster-smelling breath directly into your nostrils.

What I mean is, if you're in your bed and your dachshund isn't, you won't get any sleep. Because it will howl and whine all night long until it *is* in bed with you. And I'm serious: *all night long.*

When we first got Moxie, we were full of ideas about how she would spend the nights on her own, unlike our previous dachshund, Shortie. We filled her handsome new crate with towels and chew toys; we put it next to our bed and spoke reassuringly to Moxie whenever she whined. The first night she spent at our house, she was quite subdued. "Hey," David and I thought, "raising a puppy is easy! You just have to set limits."

The next night, Moxie woke up and cried three or four times an hour. The night after *that*, she whined, cried, and howled literally every second of the whole eight hours. (And this was the night before Laura and John started school, so we all really needed our sleep.) On the fourth night, David and I lay in bed tensely, each listening to Moxie's cries and waiting for the other to figure something out. Finally, David got up, stamped over to the crate, fiercely picked Moxie up, and stuffed her under the covers of our bed. And you know what? She cuddled right down and didn't make a sound for the rest of the night.

See what we mean? You just have to set limits.

Except that he's a coward, Beanie is better than Moxie in almost every way. Moxie has a flat head and bulging, stare-y eyes, and she doesn't recognize me if I'm wearing a sweater she hasn't seen before. Beanie has a beautiful, sensitive face like an angel's, and a head that's shaped like a head instead of a bullet. Maybe he has a bigger brain than Moxie. In fact, I'm sure he does. If you say, "Beanie, go get Moxie"—because she's hiding under a chair or something—Beanie rushes to Moxie and herds her over to us. We never taught him how to do this; he just figured it out for himself. He also figured out that if we put Moxie's leash on and don't pick it up, *he* should pick it up and drag Moxie along.

CINNAMON TOAST DOESN'T WORK OUT, LUCKILY

For a long time, Moxie was our only dog. The kids and I wanted a second dachshund, but David wasn't sure. One night I was at a choir rehearsal at my church when a man in the tenor section announced that he and his wife were trying to find a home for their son's three-legged miniature dachshund, Cinnamon Toast. The son had gone to boarding school—not that that's a good excuse for getting rid of a dog. Once you've brought a dog into your family, you should keep it! But I knew I could give Cinnamon Toast a good home, and I told the man I'd be happy to adopt him. Right after rehearsal was over, I followed the man to his house and picked up Cinnamon Toast and his bed.

I can only imagine what poor Cinnamon Toast thought about all this. To be moved from his own house at 11:00 P.M. and brought into a totally strange house where another dachshund wasn't at all pleased to see him: What was I *thinking*? The second we got home, I knew I'd made a mistake—and not only because the first thing Cinnamon Toast did was to poop on our playroom floor. But there was nothing I could do about it that night. David was already in bed, so I took the two dachshunds and tucked them into bed with me—way over on my side of the bed, of course. I figured I'd deal with it all in the morning.

When the alarm went off the next day, I said to David, "There's a surprise for you in the bed. Look under the covers."

Again, I have to ask: what was I *thinking*? Why did I imagine that David would be happy to see a fat, three-legged dachshund lying next to Moxie? He certainly laughed a lot, but it wasn't exactly joyous laughter. And when we realized that Cinnamon Toast had Moxie's same habit of peeing a little bit whenever he was patted by strangers, David said, "I won't be able to stand this."

I took Cinnamon Toast back to his real owners, who by then had realized that they, too, had made a mistake. Cinnamon Toast was so happy to see them that he wagged his whole body as he rushed back into his own house.

Anyway, we got another dog out of it. Later that day, when I was still (somehow) blaming David for the whole disaster, I blurted out, "But I only did it because we really need another dog!"

To my surprise, David said, "Fine! Fine! I just didn't want *that* other dog!" The experience must have scarred him to the point that he forgot his original objection to a second dachshund. So we got Beanie, and David adores him even more than the rest of us do. Once, I was reading the kids a book about a Scottie named Angus, and David actually found himself thinking, "I bet Beanie would *love* the Angus books."

No one would ever think of reading to Moxie. Perhaps because Moxie's brain is so tiny and useless, her body is unusually healthy. Beanie, on the other hand, is always breaking down. I'll never forget the dreadful day when we got back from vacation and I went to pick Mox and Beans up from the boarding kennel. Moxie came barking and bounding out as usual. Beanie came out dragging himself along by his front feet. He'd had a problem with his spine, and from the chest down, he had suddenly become completely paralyzed.

It was awful to see. Beanie kept confusedly turning around to stare at his back legs, as if he was asking, "Why don't you work anymore?" He obviously wasn't in pain. You could pinch one of his toes and he wouldn't even notice. But the vet said it would have been better if he *had* been hurting. The fact that Beanie felt nothing from the waist down meant he had a lot of nerve damage. He had to have an immediate operation on his spine at an animal hospital that was a long way from home.

I visited Beanie in the hospital every day. He was in a little recovery cage; it had to be small so he wouldn't move around too much and hurt his newly repaired spine. His back was shaved, and he had a tube coming out of one paw for his medication. His face was droopy with pain and sleepiness. He was glad to see me, but in a drowsy, scared way. In cages around us were other dogs, some of them whining or yelping. I would stand there patting him for fifteen minutes, and then I'd have to go. I knew that visiting him would help in his recovery, but what a hard feeling to have to leave him there over and over!

After a week, though, Beanie was allowed to come home. He was tottering and shaky and he kind of walked on tiptoe—but he was walking again. Because he still wasn't supposed to move more than necessary, I put a puppy gate around his and Moxie's bed. Every night, David would take Moxie up to sleep with him. I would arrange some sofa cushions for myself and sleep in a sleeping bag next to Beanie. He liked it best when I opened the puppy gate a little and slept with my head right on his bed.

Beanie's better now. Ever since then, though, we've had to make sure to carry him down the stairs; all that jiggling of his spine could hurt him again. We also carry Moxie, so she won't feel left out. If we don't carry her at the same time as Beanie, she runs into Laura's room and pees on the floor.

"TRAINING" MOXIE

The timing of Beanie's accident was especially bad because I had just started taking Moxie to a dog therapist to try to calm her down. For, like, ten years we were able to get along with her barking and peeing and going crazy when there was someone at the door. After her vision started to get bad, though, she became especially frantic when visitors arrived. Once, she slithered out through the door and bit a nice elderly woman in the leg before I could stop her. I decided she'd better have some real training from a professional so this wouldn't happen again.

I loved the dog doctor right away because the first thing she said was, "It wasn't Moxie's fault. Why did that woman try to come into the house when she saw how frantic Moxie was?" YES! GOOD POINT! At the same time, the doctor agreed that it wasn't a good idea to let Mox go around attacking people. (Even though she's so little and her teeth are so old.) She helped us come up with a long, detailed plan to get Moxie more and more used to strangers.

I can't remember all the details. I was supposed to teach her to sit and stay, and then to stay while I clapped my hands, and then while I jumped around in front of her, and then while I opened the door, and so on. Then, when she got really far along in her training, I was supposed to ask our friends to pretend to be guests. First, they'd come quietly into the house, ignoring Moxie. (Meanwhile, said the doctor, we should be giving Moxie "delicious treats"—like tiny scraps of cheese—to make her happier about the visitors.) When Mox could handle that, our friends would come and bang on the door and shout "Hello! Hello!" until Moxie could sit still even with that terrible activity going on right in front of her.

All of these techniques would probably have worked, too. Except that the week I was supposed to start Moxie's training was the week Beanie hurt his back. In the fuss of getting Beanie all better, Moxie's barking seemed less important. And then when we found out that Beanie would have to stay in the kitchen for several weeks while his back healed, it seemed simpler just to close Moxie in there with him. And that helped us to realize that it was really simpler just to keep Moxie from ever being able to get to the door when a stranger knocked.

Since then, life has kind of muddled along. Now that my kids are so old, I spend a lot of time alone with Moxie and Beanie. I've gotten into kind of a habit of talking to them. Aloud. (Once in a while I even talk to them when they're not in the room.) In fact, Moxie and Beanie are responsible for one of the worst things that's ever happened to me. Or are they? Some might say I'm responsible for it myself. Whoever's fault it is, here's the story.

In addition to talking to Moxie and Beanie, I also like to—I hate to say this—sing to them. Just little stupid songs about how they can't wait to have supper, or how the cat is looking in the window—stuff like that.

Anything gets turned into a song. If I see the UPS man, for instance, I might sing:

> The UPS truck's here now,
> All covered up with grime.
> Doggies, do not fear, now—
> He comes here all the time.

Or I might sing:

> There is Johnny's backpack,
> Why won't he take it up?
> I think we might trip o'er it,
> So dreadful for a pup!

I'm so used to this terribleness that I hardly notice when I start singing. One day, I had to take the dogs out to walk around the yard, and while I was putting their leashes on, I sang them a song to the tune of "Twinkle, Twinkle, Little Star." It went like this:

> Doggies' leashes are such fun,
> Doggies love to run and run.
> Doggies' leashes are such fun,
> Doggies love to run and run.
> Doggies' leashes are such fun,
> Doggies love to run and RUN!

Catchy, don't you think?

I kept on singing that song while I was out in the yard with the dogs. And—I especially hate to tell you this—I was also kind of swaying around in a little dance that if you saw *your* mom doing, you would die.

Suddenly, from up in the sky, came a man's voice. And it was really loud.

"QUIT THE SONG!"

Startled, I glanced up—and saw a man working on a telephone pole that overlooked my yard. He had been watching the whole time.

The dogs and I went back inside very, very quietly.

"That's the most embarrassing story I've ever heard," my friend Steve said later. "It makes me embarrassed to be a human being."

Well, Steve, it's what it's like to be a human being around *this* house.

THE WORST THINGS MY DOGS HAVE EATEN

Dogs will eat just about anything. They're not like cats, who sometimes won't try a new flavor of their favorite brand of cat food, even if it's advertised as being "cut into tender slices." You always hear about puppies chewing on shoes, but the things a dog will actually swallow are much, much worse. Here are a few of Beanie's and Moxie's favorite meals:

- Dead worms in the grass. The dogs like to roll on them to get that nice dead-worm perfume all over their fur. Then, time for a snack!

- Christmas ornaments. My friend once made an ornament for me, and it was boxed, wrapped, and hidden under the Christmas tree. It had been made out of flour, water, and salt, so don't tell me there was anything tempting about it.

- Moths. Beanie likes to catch them in midair.

- Ants. Beanie likes to stab at them with his snout and then lick them off his nose.

- My husband's golf caps. Maybe the sweat makes them taste good.

- Underpants.

- The head of a dead mouse left in the yard by one of my cats. Actually, Beanie didn't get a chance to swallow this. I grabbed him and turned him upsidedown and stuck my fingers down his throat and tugged the head out, while shaking Beanie with my other hand and shouting, "NO, NO, NO, NO, NO!" When I put Beanie down, I accidentally dropped the mouse head as well. Beanie almost got it *again*.

- Butter, complete with wrapper.

- Chocolate Easter eggs. One year, the kids had missed an egg during the Easter hunt. It was very small, but it made Moxie throw up for six days (chocolate is like poison for dogs). And then, if I didn't reach her in time, she would try to eat the throw-up.

- Pizza. Moxie once climbed up onto a kitchen chair and jumped onto the table to get six slices of it. She was so bloated afterward that she looked like an inner tube.

- Cat poop. The dogs will yank the leash out of my hand and crawl under the porch for this.

And let's not even get started on the things my dogs will *lick* for hours, like each other's eyes and a woolly blanket and the floor of the shower stall after someone takes a shower.

Of course, their own dog food doesn't interest them at all.

the sugar gliders

"Mom, listen to this," my daughter said one fall, when she was eight years old. She was sitting in the back seat of the car, reading the advertisements in a bird magazine. "'Sugar gliders for sale,'" she read aloud. "'Small, adorable mammals.' What's a sugar glider? Let's get one."

"Wait a minute," I said. "Let's find out a little more first. You can't rush into a thing like this."

So when we got home, Laura and I looked up sugar gliders in our big mammal guide. (This was way back in the boring days before people could go online to find out stuff.) "OH!" we screamed in unison as soon as we found the right page. The sugar

gliders in the picture were very, very cute—chipmunk-sized, with round, immense black eyes and velvety-soft gray fur. Their tails curled like question marks.

I decided right away that I would get Laura a pair of sugar gliders for Christmas. That's what I call not rushing into things.

This was more than ten years ago, when sugar gliders weren't nearly as well known as they are now. You've probably seen a sugar glider; you may even have a friend who owns one. But back then I had never heard of sugar gliders, and the breeder who was selling them lived in San Diego, California. I live in Connecticut, so I couldn't just hop into the car and pick them up. They would have to be shipped cross-country—and they would have to be shipped early, so they could settle in before Christmas.

I called my friends Jim and Jane, who lived around the corner from my house. "Um, guys?" I said. "Can I have a Christmas present for Laura shipped to your house so she won't see it?"

"Of course!" Jim and Jane said. "What is it?"

"It's an animal. Well, two animals."

"Uh . . . fine. No problem!"

"And also, they won't be weaned, so I'll have to come over every couple of hours to feed them their formula. Including last thing at night and first thing in the morning."

"Oh, yeah, right," Jim and Jane should have said. *"That's really going to be convenient for us, a few days before Christmas—you trotting in and out all the time with jars of formula."*

But they were very gracious about it, and on Christmas morning Laura had her surprise. And there's no way it could have been a surprise if I'd tried to hide the babies in my own house. Sugar gliders make a funny squawking sound that any kid on the alert for a hidden animal would have noticed in a second. Plus, they have a very special, well, smell.

Speaking of smells, let's get one animal topic out of the way right now: **POOP**.

I'm going to call it "poop" in this book, rather than something science-y like "manure" or "droppings." Poop is what I think of as the real word. (If you say something

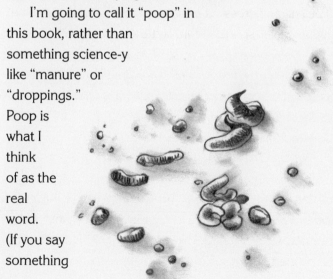

more polite like "number two" or "doody," I'm sorry to gross you out.)

If you love animals, there's no way you can avoid talking about poop, and thinking about it, and cleaning it up all the time. The only person I know whose pet never caused a "poop problem" was my friend Banjie, who had a tame hummingbird that had been hurt and couldn't be released into the wild. Ruby, the humming-bird, flew all over the house, but her poops were so tiny that no one noticed or cared about them. It would have been different if she'd been an ostrich.

Actually, the problem with sugar gliders isn't their poop, though there's plenty of that. It's their pee. Sugar glider pee smells like turpentine with Froot Loops cereal stirred in. Many small mammals pee in one corner of their cages—as a way to sort of keep things tidy—but sugar gliders pee from high up in their cages, the way they'd pee from the treetops if they lived in the wild. So the pee sprays everywhere and the bars of their cage always get sticky.

My son's friend Willie, who was about six, wouldn't even play in our playroom once we got the sugar gliders. "I hate that smell," he said. And when a six-year-old boy won't go into a room, you *know* it smells bad.

But let me get back to talking about Sam and Sapphire themselves, because believe me, there will be plenty of other chances to talk about animal poop in this book.

Since they had been hand raised, they were very tame. If they heard us walking toward their cage, they'd squawk and start leaping around and running upside down on the top of their cage. Gliders have flaps of skin between their front and back legs that act like parachutes and let them sail through the air. In the wild, they can glide as far as 400 feet. In our house, of course, they couldn't do that, but we did let them leap around the playroom. They loved to be carried around in our cupped hands and would settle right down to sleep. They also loved to run up and down our arms and around our necks. Probably the best thing to wear if you're letting a sugar glider climb on you is a hooded sweatshirt. A sugar glider's claws are quite sharp, and I often got a rash on my skin where they'd scratched me. But the thought that such an unusual animal was treating me like a tree was worth the scratches. Getting scratched is another thing besides poop that you have to get used to if you own a bunch of animals.

One of the best things about sugar gliders is that—like many animals from Australia—they're marsupials. In other words, the females raise their babies in a pouch. (Quick, kids, what is the only marsupial native to North America? That's right: the opossum.) One or two babies are born, very tiny and undeveloped, after sixteen days of pregnancy. They crawl into the pouch, attach themselves to a nipple, and stay there for the next few weeks while they grow. You couldn't see Sapphire's pouch; it was under her fur. But we all hoped that one day it would be bulging with babies.

This will sound like almost too much of a coincidence, but the next Christmas after we'd gotten Sam and Sapphire, we noticed that Sapphy's stomach *was* looking bulgy. We knew this meant there were babies in there, and we couldn't wait to see their little heads peeking out at us.

Unfortunately, the first sign we saw of the babies was a dead one lying on the floor of the cage. And without going into details, let me say that he was really very, very dead. "Oh, my God," I muttered under my breath—and Laura and John, who had been peeking over my shoulder, were out of the room in a single leap as if they themselves were sugar gliders. I pulled the tiny form out of the cage, wishing—as always—that my *own* mother were there to do it for me. (There are some jobs you just never grow up enough to be able to do without cringing.) "Well, kids," I said to Laura and John, who were cowering in the next room, "I guess we won't have baby sugar gliders after all."

"Did Sapphire push him out of the pouch?" Laura asked timidly.

"Either that, or he died and she had to get him out of there, or he was climbing on her back and he fell. We'll probably never know." I sighed. "I'm sorry, guys. She still looks bulgy, so maybe she's got another baby in there."

She did. The next morning, when we were about to leave for church, we checked the sugar gliders' cage again. My stomach lurched. There, on the floor of the cage, was another baby sugar glider. Sapphire had had two babies, and now they were both dead.

But wait! This baby was still breathing! Shrinking back, I reached in and picked him up.

The baby was about the length of my thumb and hardly much fatter. A thin layer of velvety gray fuzz coated his back, but his stomach was still bare and pink like a baby mouse's. No belly button, of course, because of his being a marsupial. His eyes were closed, and his tail formed a thin spiral. And he was definitely breathing.

"Go see if we have any pet formula left," I said to Laura.

"But, Mom—church!" I was John and Laura's Sunday school teacher, so I did usually try to be on time.

"We'll have to be a little late," I said. "I'm sure the other kids won't mind when they see this baby."

Let me interrupt myself to talk about pet formula for a second. It's a great thing to have on hand. You can buy it powdered and add water to it, or you can buy it ready-made. I usually buy the powdered kind because it's cheaper and I only need to use a small amount at a time. And I always keep kitten and puppy formulas in the freezer (along with baby-bird formula), just in case.

I didn't have an eyedropper in the house, so I dipped a cotton swab into the formula and held it up to the baby's mouth. He grabbed the swab in his teeny hands and began lapping at it with a tongue that couldn't have been any bigger than a clipped-off pinky fingernail. In a few seconds, you could actually see the milk inside his stomach—that's how thin his skin was. A few seconds more and his pink tummy was rounded and bulging. Maybe this was going to work!

"Okay, kids," I said. "Let's take him to church."

I couldn't teach much of a Sunday school class that day. All the kids just wanted to hold the baby glider. Why do people always want to *hold* animals? Whenever anyone sees my pets, they always ask if they can pick them up. Some kids even ask if they can pick up my birds. Why isn't it enough just to watch the animal and maybe pat it a little if that won't scare it? Would *we* like being picked up and carried around by a total stranger? When I'm president, this is the first thing I'm going to outlaw. In any case, Nutcracker was way too small and fragile to be passed around. I did let the kids pat him with a fingertip, but that was all.

I could see already that this was going to be a challenge. Holding Nutcracker as much as possible would be the closest thing to keeping him in a pouch. But it would mean I couldn't get much done with my left hand—especially typing. I decided it would be easiest to wear a soft stretchy glove on that hand and tuck Nutcracker into my palm. That way I'd still be able to use my fingers, though of course I would have to be careful. No carrying suitcases or cactuses! No dishwashing! When I had to, I put Nutcracker in a small cage with a heating pad. But I kept him inside the glove as much as possible.

Nutcracker was so little that he slept most of the time. When I could feel him start to squirm in my palm, I knew it was time to feed him. (I knew it was time to wash my hand when I could feel him peeing.) At night I kept him in his cage on a heating pad in my bedroom, waking up every two hours to feed him. After the first night, Nutcracker recognized what the sound of the alarm clock meant. He'd start making his little squawky rumbling noise to call me while I fumbled around trying to find the clock and turn off the alarm. And he'd be sitting up in his cage when I sleepily brought him his formula.

It took Nutcracker a month and a half before he was completely weaned off formula. After two weeks, he was too big to fit into the glove. He had enough fur to keep himself warm on his own, so I kept him in his cage most of the time. As soon as he was eating solid food, I put him back in the big cage with Sam and Sapphire.

Sam and Sapphire had three more babies, and they never got much better at raising them. I hand raised the babies in the same way—well, almost. The second time around, I realized that if I lined my—I'm sorry to mention this—my bra with paper towel, I could keep the baby in there. This let me use both hands normally. All I had to do was persuade myself that it wasn't that big a deal and remember not to reach down into my shirt to check on the baby in public.

For all kinds of reasons, I'm sorry to say that one of my grandfathers died while I was hand raising a baby glider. The memorial service was out of town, and the baby was still too young to leave on her own. I was afraid to leave her in the hotel room; pets weren't allowed in that hotel. Maybe a caged animal didn't count as a "pet," but I didn't know what would happen to the baby if a hotel housekeeper found her. So—you guessed it— she came to the church in my bra. I don't think anyone noticed, and the one time the baby made her clucking "I'm hungry" sound, it wasn't too loud. If anyone heard her, maybe they just thought it was my stomach rumbling. At the reception after the memorial service, I was careful not to hug any of my relatives too tightly.

I'm sure God didn't mind, but my grandfather might have. I'm sorry, Grandpa, but what else could I do?

japan

"I can't believe you're not taking me and the kids along with you," I said to David.

"It's a *work* trip," he insisted. "I'm going to be doing *research*."

"I don't see how going to Scotland to play golf counts as research," I said—but I knew it was a losing battle. My husband writes a lot about golf. Even *I* realize that you can't write about golf without playing it.

Still, a trip to Scotland—a place I'd always wanted to go—seemed like an unfair amount of fun to me. Why couldn't David just write about a golf course in the next town?

"Have a great time," I said sourly. "But I want you to know that when you come home, there's going to be a bird in the house."

By this time, we already owned a bunch of mammals, including a vole and a hedgehog. But a bird seemed to be crossing some kind of line. Except for a couple of fish and an albino frog, we had never owned a nonmammal. In theory, I loved birds—but close up, I didn't like looking at their beaks and their scaly feet.

That was before I saw the cockatiel.

Now, I try never to go into pet stores. They make me too sad. There are some good ones out there, but way more terrible ones. It's dreadful to see pets crammed into too-small cages and to know that if they're not sold they may be killed or worse. And so many of the people who visit pet stores are such morons! Banging on the glass, screaming, "Come out! Come out!" and sometimes even reaching into cages to grab some poor frightened animal. . . . It always makes me wish they'd get bitten or pecked. That would teach 'em. Or maybe it wouldn't. Maybe people like that would just sue the store. Anyway, as I say, I try never to go to pet stores. I buy my own pets' supplies online or at feed stores where they don't sell any animals.

Every now and then, though, I run out of hamster food or something and have no choice but to visit a pet store. It was on one such visit that I noticed a cage with a cockatiel in it who seemed to be looking right at me.

"Hey, wait a minute!" I thought. "He really *is* looking right at me! He wants me to come over!"

The cockatiel was weaving and swaying in a most

inviting way, almost as if he was dancing. He shimmied even harder as I walked over.

"Hi, guy," I said. (My kids were little then, so they weren't embarrassed that I was talking to a bird in public.) The cockatiel cocked his head, then bobbed it up and down while shifting eagerly from foot to foot. If he could have talked, I'm certain he would have been saying, "Hi! Hi! It's great to see you! Let me out! Hi! I'm so glad to get some attention! Hi! How are you?"

I didn't buy him, but I didn't stop thinking about him either.

"No birds," David said to me just before he left for Scotland. He didn't know that I'd already called a cockatiel breeder. The next day, I went to visit her. I wouldn't mind being a bird breeder. And actually, since my canaries and finches have babies all the time, I guess I kind of *am* one—but not one like Sheri. In Sheri's house there were two parrots in a huge aviary in her living room. One, named Ruffy, made a gobbling noise when he saw me. His voice sounded like a jar of walnuts being shaken and then thrown down the stairs.

"Ruffy, that's not clear," said Sheri sternly.

Ruffy uttered a different stream of sounds. His muttering still didn't sound like words, but it sounded more human. "He's still working on his talking," Sheri explained. I decided that even if he never learned to talk,

Ruffy could at least learn to sound like the kind of person who's always grumbling and complaining under his breath.

Sheri's bird room was much warmer than the rest of the house. (Birds like warmer temperatures than most people do.) In one corner of the room was an incubator full of different kinds of eggs, each pencilled with the date it was supposed to hatch. I was very jealous of this. In fourth grade, I built an incubator with my dad, using a cardboard box and a lightbulb. But Sheri's incubator looked magical to me, like something an emperor would own. It even had racks that turned the eggs every two hours so that they'd heat evenly.

And then there was a clutch of baby cockatiels in a big cage in one corner—and one of them was Japan. He was eight weeks old, with a pale yellow crest on his head that tremblingly rose and fell as he looked at me. The rest of his feathers were white, yellow, and gray, except for his face: he had a bright reddish orange circle on each cheek that reminded me of the Japanese flag.

Sheri held her index finger out like a little perch and nudged Japan's stomach with it. "Up, up," she told him. Obediently, he climbed up onto the finger and stood there looking from side to side. His neck was stretched way out—because he was scared, Sheri said. But anyone could see he was interested in having a new person in the room.

"I'm just looking for now," I had told Sheri on the phone. But of course I ended up buying Japan. I had no choice, did I?

"So," my husband said disgustedly when I told him the news on the phone that night. "Now we're the kind of family that has a *bird*."

I don't know what he was so upset about. It's true that for the first few days in our house, Japan whistled and whooped a lot whenever he was alone. But after a while he calmed down. What I mean is, after a while we got used to his screaming, except of course for my husband. Anyway, it wasn't all *that* loud.

The funny thing was that although Japan liked me, he adored David. Whenever David walked into the room, Japan would scream with excitement, fly to the front of his cage, and scramble all over the bars trying to get David to notice him. This didn't impress David much, since Japan also fell in love with a pair of yellow rubber gloves I wore to wash the dishes. Whenever I put on the gloves and held them up to the cage, Japan would coo and sway around like a hula dancer. It was one of the many, many times I've wished I could exchange brains with an animal to find out exactly what he's thinking.

And Japan had some fascinating hobbies. Fascinating to him, anyway; to a human, they might not be quite so riveting. One of his favorite activities was pulling the stoppers out of the bottoms of Bic ballpoint pens. Whenever I showed him a pen, he would rush up and start prying the stopper out with his beak. I think he would have done it five hundred times in a row if I had let him.

He also loved playing with toothpicks. I would make a pile of toothpicks on the kitchen table and turn him loose. He would eagerly pick up each toothpick, carry it to the edge of the table, and drop it onto the floor. Why? Did he think he was accomplishing something? I could never figure it out. The good thing about the game from my point of view was that I could keep reading the newspaper while Japan did his "toothpick work."

Japan loved to walk around on the kitchen table. I let him do it because it seemed like the kind of thing most parents would never allow. This made me feel like a modern, relaxed mom. Once, Japan ran right through a plate of seven-layer dip when we had house-guests, but luckily they weren't the kind of friends who cared about stuff like that.

Sheri had warned me never to let Japan climb up my arm onto my shoulder; she said that if he got used to being so high up, he would never be content just to perch on my hand. But I enjoyed carrying him around on my shoulder. His wings were clipped, so he couldn't fly away. (Once, though, he *blew* off my shoulder when we were outside in the yard. After that, I never took him outside again.) There were only two problems with carrying him around this way. First, he pooped on my back sometimes. I solved this by draping a dish towel over my shoulder and making him stand on that, but I didn't care about it too much. If you really like small animals, as I've said, you just have to get used to poop.

More annoying was that if I was wearing earrings, Japan would instantly start trying to take them off. His "work" with the ballpoint pens gave him a lot of practice, and he became quite good at pulling off post earrings and dropping them on the ground. That didn't hurt too much. What *did* hurt was when Japan would start yanking my hoop earrings. Someone should invent a bird toy that sits on your shoulder between the bird and your ear. Maybe it could be attached to an anti-poop shoulder cape.

Some cockatiels can learn to talk, but Japan never did. He was great at imitating the microwave oven, though. And, it turned out, he was also great at imitating a parent bird. When he was about two years old, I decided to get a large cage and move Japan and my two parakeets into it. Even though Japan was a different species, I figured he'd prefer the company of other birds. But as soon as he'd been moved into the new cage, he began throwing up all over the place.

Did he hate his new cagemates? Was he so nervous being around strange birds that he couldn't keep his food down? I got worried enough that I finally called Sheri.

"He thinks of them as his babies," she said.

Excuse me? He's throwing up because he thinks of them as his babies?

Exactly, Sheri explained. A mother or father bird will regurgitate (a fancy word for "throw up") its food to feed its babies. Japan wanted to take care of the new, smaller birds, and this was the only way he knew how to do it.

Of course the parakeets, being neither babies nor cockatiels, were uninterested in piles of Japan's vomit, and in a couple of days he stopped throwing up. He was definitely much happier having roommates, and as I added more birds he loved being the boss of the cage. (The littler birds would let him eat first.) I stopped clipping his wings so that he'd be able to fly around, and he loved that, too. Japan became best friends with the parakeet that looked the most like him, but he didn't forget about me. Whenever he heard my steps coming into the room, he would whistle and rush to the front of

his perch to wait for me. Then, in a burst of clucks and chirps, he would tell me all the bird gossip.

Japan died after many years, and I buried him in the garden. Quaker, my bulbul, lives in Japan's old cage. Unlike Japan, Quaker was so mean to all the littler birds that I had to move them to a cage of their own. Quaker has her charms (although I'm not always sure what they are), and I'll tell you about them in another chapter— but Japan will always be king of the birds to me.

Hey, wait! I've *still* never been to Scotland! That's very sad. Do you think I should get some kind of pet to cheer myself up?

the pygmy mice

Pygmy mice are the smallest kind of mouse there is. They're even smaller than the period at the end of this sentence.

No, not really. I just wanted to say that. But pygmy mice *are* very, very small. Their Latin name, *Mus minutoides,* means "the smallest mouse." Newborn, they're the size of honeybees. Fully grown, they're only two inches long (not counting the tail, of course.) They make regular-sized mice look like cows.

I love, love, love everything miniature. To me, anything nice is a hundred percent nicer if it's miniature. In my spare time, I'm building a miniature store filled with miniature supplies and tiny, tiny foods. When I make chocolates (because that's another great thing about being an adult—you can buy yourself a chocolate-dipping machine), I always make them half-size. Two of my rabbits are dwarfs; even their ears are much shorter than regular rabbits' ears. My dogs are miniature dachshunds, and I've never understood why there can't be miniature cats. They would be so adorable!

So when I saw my first pygmy mice, I was thrilled. I couldn't believe something that delicate and perfect existed. Pygmy mice are brown with white undersides and twinkling, dainty feet. You don't get to see them very often; they live in tunnels and they come out only at night. But that makes them seem even more magical.

Pygmy mice originally come from Africa. I've read that tribal peoples used to notice the mice gathering tiny pebbles and placing them at the entrance to their tunnels. In the early morning, dew would collect on the pebbles, and the mice would drink it. Because of this, one of their nicknames in Africa is pebble herdsmen. I've tried giving my mice small pebbles, but they never do anything with them. Maybe that's because they have plenty of water in their water bottles.

Pygmy mice aren't very common as pets in the United States. I suspect that many people aren't interested in them; they are too shy really to count as pets. You can be as nice as you want to a pygmy mouse, but it will *never* become tame. It will *always* dart from your hand in panic if you reach toward it. A tank of pygmy mice is more like a collection of insects than a collection of pets, especially because the mice build antlike tunnels and can jump as high as grasshoppers when they're scared. The nicest thing you can do for them is to give them plenty of space and some nice deep bedding to burrow in—and then leave them alone. You'll hardly ever see the mice. They won't come out during the day. But you'll know they're there, and you can watch them playing at night if you're willing to sit in the dark. That's way more fun than trying to pat them or carry them around.

At night I turn out all the lights in the room where I keep my tanks of pygmy mice. I leave one light on out in the hall: the mice can see fine in total darkness, but I can't. Plugging in a nightlight would also work— anything that casts a dim enough glow that the mice won't be frightened and stay hidden. (I keep meaning to try one of those red lightbulbs that zoos use for their nocturnal animals, but I haven't gotten around to it yet.) Feeling like Fern in *Charlotte's Web*, I pull up a chair and settle down to watch Pygmy Mouse TV.

One by one, the mice emerge from their tunnels. Stretching and yawning—such amazingly tiny yawns!— they begin on their night work. Several of them will jump onto their exercise wheel. Even the smallest-sized exercise wheel is big enough for four pygmy mice at once, though they have a little trouble if half of them decide to run in one direction and half in the other. Sometimes a couple of mice will get a running start on the wheel, and another mouse, unprepared, will be carried all the way around upside down. They never seem to mind, though.

Meanwhile, other pygmies are scampering around the rooms of the tiny plastic houses I've given them. For some reason, they like to jump out of the windows of their houses over and over. Even though it's only a couple of inches to the floor of their tank, and they couldn't possibly get hurt, they always carefully look down before they jump. Why does that seem so cute?

I feed my pygmy mice the smallest birdseed I can find. Still, one seed in his mouth makes a pygmy mouse's cheeks bulge as if he had stuffed them. I put a couple of orange segments in each tank; each segment will last for at least a week. Sometimes I put in a chunk of corn on the cob as well. Three or four mice will work

on the corn at once, but it takes them at least a week to finish all the kernels. Every time I clean their cages, I give them a dog biscuit; that way, they'll have something extra hard to gnaw on. As the month goes by, their tiny tooth scrapings round off the ends and edges of the biscuit. But they can never finish it.

Speaking of cage cleaning, that's one nice thing about pygmy mice. Unlike hamsters and guinea pigs and other rodents, their cages don't need to be cleaned very often. Every six weeks or so, I listen to an audiobook while I clean the mouse tanks. I have to scoop out the dirty bedding with my hands; it's the only way to be sure I don't throw a mouse away by mistake. Once or twice, I've scooped up a mouse along with the bedding and thrown it into the garbage. Then I've had to start all over, scooping up the dirty bedding from the garbage bag and putting it into *another* garbage bag. Only the mouse is left in the garbage bag at the end of this process. I gently shake him back into the clean tank. Then I go wash my hands.

As I'm scooping up the top layer of bedding in the tank, the lower layers begin to bubble up as if there's an earthquake. That's the mice waking up. They're just beginning to realize that their world is disappearing. They pile on top of one another, hoping that will protect them. I try to gather up all the bedding around them to leave them their security for as long as possible. But at last I have to lift the newsprint shavings that cover them. The mice blink up at me and dart in all directions. Some stand in corners, frantically washing their faces. (That's how rodents make themselves feel secure.) Some try to burrow under ridiculously small pieces of bedding. They seem to think that if I can't see their faces, they'll be okay. I wipe the bottom of the tank with a piece of wet paper towel and put in the new shavings as fast as I can. When I'm all done, the mice start working on a new complex of tunnels.

As I said earlier, pygmy mice are hard to find in this country. A couple of years ago, I had six of them—two males and four females—shipped to me from a breeder in Illinois. I don't normally buy pets that need airplane shipping, but I knew the mice could handle it because their breeder was going to pack them very, very carefully, and it was going to be a short flight. I drove an hour and a half to the airport cargo area to pick them up. It was all I could do to keep myself from opening their shipping crate in my car, but I forced myself to wait. If the mice escaped in my car, I'd never see them again.

I didn't realize at first how much space pygmy mice need, especially males. One thing that's definitely not cute about them is that the males fight constantly if they don't have a big-enough territory. In a tank that's too small, a group of males may pick on one poor male relentlessly. They'll bite off chunks of his ears and tail and even rip patches of fur off his legs. Giving the males enough space reduces their fights, but even so, they may choose to pick on an older or weaker male in the bunch. When one of the males starts spending his time out in the open during the day, it's pretty likely that he's being picked on; he would never choose to be above-ground otherwise. If you don't give him a tank all to himself, the other males may actually kill him.

I have two ten-gallon glass aquariums with five males in each, and a small plastic tank where one abused male, Walter, lives by himself. Poor Walter had had his tail bitten almost completely off when I found him one morning. He recovered quickly once he was on his own, but I'm afraid to put him back into one of the larger tanks. Animals have a way of picking on weaker members of their community. It's hard not to hate them for this, but the behavior is so common among certain animal species that you just have to understand it and take preventive measures. It's the animals' instinctive way of protecting themselves against predators: a weakened or sick member will draw attention to the whole group. So I'm afraid Walter will have to live out his days alone.

Walter has his own exercise wheel and a tiny flower pot to use as a house, and he seems content to tunnel around alone. Mysteriously, his tail seems to be growing back. I know that's impossible—mammals *can't* regenerate missing body parts!—and yet every time I clean Walter's cage, his tail seems slightly longer to me. I'm going to start taking pictures of him to check this out. As I say, I must be imagining things, but . . .

I may give Walter a female companion at some point. My fourteen female pygmy mice live very happily in one tank, with no fights. Meanwhile, the fifteenth female lives very happily somewhere in my house, because she escaped from the tank when I was showing the mice to some girls named Lizzy and Daisy. The mouse ran right between Lizzy's feet and vanished. (Being a sensible girl, Lizzy just moved her heels apart slightly so the mouse could run through. She didn't scream or jump or do anything that might have hurt the mouse.) I did see the mouse a month later. She was tiptoeing into the finches' cage and helping herself to some of their spilled birdseed. So I knew she had figured out how to take care of herself.

I wondered for a second about letting all my pygmy mice go free. If I kept food out on the floor for them, they'd never starve. And they'd have more and more babies, and soon the walls of my house would be magically filled with miniature mice instead of the regular house mice they're filled with now. But that idea was too crazy even for me.

Speaking of more and more babies, have you noticed something about the numbers in this chapter? I said I started out with six mice. Now I'm talking about a total of twenty-six. Why do you think I put the males and females in separate tanks? And if I do put a female in with Walter—well—do you know anyone who wants baby pygmy mice?

the baby bat

The baby bat's story is a sad one. It happened a long time ago, before I knew much about wild animals. But if you love animals, there's a lot you can learn from it. Before I get started, let me tell you a little about bats—because if you don't like them, I *insist* that you change your mind.

People have weird ideas about bats. They believe that all bats are vampires. They also believe that bats like to fly into your hair. That's silly. Why would *any* animal want to fly into someone's hair? And although vampire bats do exist, they don't live in the United States. And they don't attack people anyway. And even if they did, I would still like them. It's not their fault that they need to drink blood to survive. They have as much right to drink blood as we have to drink milk. They're welcome to some of my blood anytime. It's not as if they're going to empty me out.

The bats in the United States won't hurt anyone except mosquitoes. Bats are *great* at eating mosquitoes and other annoying insects. One little brown bat can eat 1,200 mosquitoes an hour! And a colony of big brown bats can eat 33 *million* rootworms in a summer. That helps farmers protect their crops. We should all be building bat houses on our property, not worrying about bats getting into our hair.

But back to my *own* baby bat—mine for a few hours anyway.

I live out in the country. Bats swoop and dive through the air above my house every summer night. Now and then, one of them gets into the house. That's not much fun for any of us. A bat got into my daughter's bedroom once, when she was a baby, and kept flying over her crib. "Moth in room!" Laura screamed.

Then she got a closer look. "ANIMAL in room!" she screamed even louder.

We had to chase the bat outside by flapping a towel at it, while it flew around and around and around the downstairs of the house. And I do have to confess that although I knew it wouldn't get in my hair, it flew so close to my head that I couldn't help ducking whenever it passed.

I had always wanted to see a bat up close, and one day I got my chance. My friend Banjie is licensed by the state to take care of all kinds of baby birds. Whenever anyone in our town finds a baby bird, he or she takes it to Banjie. She has helped to save all kinds of birds—from hummingbirds to bluebirds to crows. Sometimes she has four different kinds of babies at once. Last summer, she raised three baby woodpeckers in a hollow log who screamed all day long without stopping. (The birds, not the log.)

But Banjie doesn't work with wild baby mammals. One afternoon she called to tell me that she had noticed a baby bat huddled on a log in her back yard. For two days the tiny baby had been there, and no adult bats had come near it. "Do you want to take a look at it?" she asked me.

Of course I said yes. But it didn't turn out quite the way I had hoped.

I was in my kitchen when Banjie brought in the baby bat. The minute she walked into the house—while she was still standing out in the hall—I smelled something just terrible. Sort of a garbage-y smell, sort of a bathroom-y smell that filled the whole downstairs of my house.

And the smell was coming from the tiny bat in Banjie's hand.

There was another problem besides the smell. In my imagination, baby bats were cute. I thought of them as field mice with wings, even though I'd seen pictures of them and they actually look nothing like mice. This bat was not cute. Interesting, but not cute. I had to force myself to look closely at him. He was maybe two inches long, not counting his wings. The wings were folded up, and the bat twitched weakly. His eyes were closed. His face looked like a dog's head with Frankenstein teeth. And he was crawling with mites.

Well. You can't say you don't want to help a baby bat just because it stinks and it's covered with bugs. That's not the bat's fault, is it? So I held out the little cage I'd

prepared for the bat, and Banjie left. I hope she washed her hands for a long time when she got home.

Before I could even feed the poor thing, I had to try to get rid of those mites. After all, I was going to be holding that bat a lot. Baby animals need warmth almost as much as they need food. In the wild, this happens when they cuddle next to their mothers. Since this bat's mother was not in the picture, I would have to do the cuddling myself.

I dusted the bat with a mixture of cornstarch and flea powder. That, I hoped, would take care of the bugs. (It's what you do for wild baby birds with mites.)

Then I made up a small bowl of kitten formula. (Kitten formula can also be used for baby raccoons, guinea pigs, hamsters, gerbils, chipmunks, and opossums. Puppy formula can be used for baby squirrels, ferrets, skunks, rats, and rabbits. Why can't kitten formula be used for squirrels? I guess only science can answer that.) I dipped a cotton swab into the formula and tried to get the bat interested.

He opened his mouth the minute he smelled the formula, but I couldn't seem to figure out how to make him suck the swab. His tiny, pin-sharp teeth kept sticking to the cotton. "Why do you *have* teeth this early?" I wanted to say. "You're too young for teeth! They're just getting in my way!"

After a few minutes, I decided it wasn't working. I would have to take the bat to a nature center. I hoped someone there would be able to tell me how to find someone who could help.

Tucking a tiny mammal inside a glove, as I did with the first baby sugar glider I raised, keeps the baby warm enough to get through the day. I can't use the glove when I'm sleeping, of course, and I can't use it when I'm driving. So I took a sock, hung it on a string around my neck, and gently dropped the bat inside. Then I tucked the sock inside my shirt and started off for the nature center.

It was going to be a long drive—about an hour. I could feel the bat squirming. It tickled, but I didn't mind. The squirming told me the bat was still lively.

Halfway to the nature center, the squirming stopped. I pulled my car to the side of the road to look inside the sock. I knew what I would find, and that's what I *did* find. The baby bat had died.

Why? I'll never know. But an awful lot had happened to that bat in the previous couple of hours. He had been picked up by human hands and carried to my house. He had had a flea bath. (Nothing in the wild could have prepared him for that!) He had tried to eat and failed. All of this must have stressed him out a lot. Sometimes, when animals are too stressed, their hearts simply stop.

Driving along with a dead bat inside my shirt is not the kind of thing even *I* like to do! But, if you love wild animals, you can't let yourself be squeamish. I had done the best I could for the bat. Maybe I would never get to see another baby bat up close. If I did, maybe I would know better how to help it.

As I said, this happened before I knew much about wild animals. I've learned a few things since then, and now I know that I made a lot of mistakes with the bat.

First of all, remember that the bat had been alone for two days? That should have told me his chances were bad. A very young animal needs to eat all day long. If he hasn't been fed for two days, he's in big trouble. Probably there was nothing I could have done to save the bat at that point. It might have been better to leave him where he was. Certainly that would have scared him less. He would have been outside, where he felt more comfortable. And no one would have been picking him up and poking at him.

More important, I should have called a wildlife center the minute I heard about the bat. A trained wildlife expert almost always knows more than even the most devoted animal lover. In most of the United States, it's against the law to take care of a baby wild animal yourself. You need a special license to care for wild animals, and you need to pass special tests to get that license.

Maybe nothing much could have been done to save the bat. But a wildlife expert would still have known much more than I did. If you ever find a baby wild animal, don't touch it! Leave it where it is and call a nature center or animal-control officer to ask what to do.

I can't be completely sorry about my bat story. I still love bats. And now, when I see them swooping overhead, I feel closer to them than I did before.

THE ONLY PETS MY HUSBAND
EVER BROUGHT US

When John was about a week old, David came home from shopping to find that John was crying, three-and-a-half-year-old Laura was crying, and I was crying because both children were crying. The dog was probably crying, too. David backed out of the house, backed the car out of the driveway, and disappeared for quite some time. When he returned, he said, "Laura, I have a present for you!"

Laura rushed up to see what he was unpacking. It turned out to be an aquarium and two fancy gold-

fish. One was black, the other orange and white. They had swishy, ruffly fins and huge, bulging eyes.

"I hope *you're* planning to take care of them," I told David rudely. The thought of cleaning an aquarium with a newborn baby in the house seemed unwelcome to me.

Laura was much happier to see the new pets than I was. She watched eagerly as David set up the aquarium and slid the two fish out of their plastic bag into the water. As soon as the fish began swimming around their new home, Laura said, "I want to hold them!"

"Oh, no, no. You can't hold fish, honey," her dad told her. "They need to stay in the water."

Instant meltdown. "Then I hate them! I want you to *cook* them!" Laura commanded.

Eventually she got over her disappointment, and the two fish—named Bulgy and Puffy—became part of the household. Not a very interesting part, but at least David took care of the tank. And as soon as John was able to crawl, he loved to pull himself up and show the fish his Duplo bricks.

Bulgy and Puffy joined us in January. A month or so later, we added some ordinary goldfish to the tank to be their friends. That spring, David took Laura and her friend Emily wading in a nearby river. The girls came home very excited, carrying a tiny crayfish David had found under a rock.

"We can put him in the tank with the fish," David said.

It was fun to watch him there. Crayfish—in case you've never seen one—look exactly like miniature lobsters. Crayfishy was tiny, maybe an inch and a half long. For a couple of days he zoomed energetically around the tank. Then we came into the playroom on the third morning to find that Crayfishy had killed Puffy. He had also eaten Puffy's eyes.

Feeling sick, David took Puffy's body out of the tank. "At least Crayfishy's not hungry anymore," he said gloomily.

That afternoon Laura, Emily, John, and I were playing in our playroom. John was staggering around holding on to my hands when the girls suddenly began screaming.

"Crayfishy caught Bulgy! Crayfishy caught Bulgy!" they shrieked.

It was true. Crayfishy had leapt up through the water and grabbed Bulgy by the tail. Though he was much smaller than the fish, he was whipping Bulgy back and forth like a flag.

"Girls, go out to the porch," I said. While Laura and Emily cowered out of sight, I reached into the tank, trembling, to see if I could pull Bulgy free.

Instantly, all the other goldfish in the tank swam up and started nibbling on my hand. Meanwhile, John had crawled over and was grabbing the backs of my legs, trying to hoist himself up. Somehow I managed to ignore him and the nibbling fish and to peel Bulgy loose from Crayfishy's tiny claws. But it was clear that Bulgy had been hurt too badly to survive.

Crayfishy went back to the river that same day, and David never brought home another animal—until he got Snips, our turtle. But that was much later, and Snips is in another chapter. And anyway, we all loved Snips (except for David).

the rats

If there's anything I hate, it's people who hate rats. I hate those people even more than people who hate bats.

I hate people who hate rodents, period. I was once at a party where a woman was saying that her daughter had asked for a hamster. "I said, 'No, honey. Hamsters are *rodents*,'" the woman said to me. Boy, was she telling this to the wrong person!

Anyone who doesn't like rats is missing out on a very nice animal. I'm not talking about wild rats, the kind that live in city buildings and barns and do lots of damage. I understand that rats in the Middle Ages spread the plague and that people might feel a little squeamish about catching the plague. Even though it's actually fleas that spread plague, not rats.

When I was a little girl, a wild rat got into our house. He would climb up onto the kitchen table and eat the skin off the pears my mom kept there in a bowl. My mother thought my little sister was doing it. "Nelie, if you want a pear, you should take a *whole* pear," said my mother.

"But I don't *like* pears!" protested Nelie.

Eventually, we saw the rat outside eating birdseed from under the birdfeeder, and my dad decreed that he would have to be poisoned. But when my mother and I found his little dead body out in the garage, we both had tears in our eyes. We covered him up with a piece of newspaper and made Dad deal with him when he got home from work.

Lots of people think a rat's long, naked tail is ugly. But I bet if you asked a rat, she would say that humans' long, thick legs are disgusting.

More to the point, tame rats make wonderful pets.

In my family we think pet rats are nice—tails and all. Most of the rats you'll find in a pet store are either black and white or all-white. But pet rats come in lots of colors and types, just like hamsters (and people). You can get fancy rats with big ears—dumbo rats, they're called—or curly fur, or satiny fur, or even no fur at all. You can get rats without tails, though I don't see the point of that.

Whatever kind you get, you'll be getting a pet who loves company, loves being handled, and loves playing. Rats are awake during the day, unlike many rodents. When a pet rat hears you coming into the room, it will jump up and rush to the side of its cage to see you. You can train a pet rat to play tug-of-war with a piece of string and to come when you call it. Rats like being carried around in their owners' pockets or on their shoulders. (Carrying a rat on your shoulder is especially fun because it bothers other people.)

When Laura was four, she asked Santa for a pet rat for Christmas. On Christmas Eve, she said to her dad, "I can't wait to play with that rat tomorrow!"

"You'd better wait and see if Santa brings it," said David. "Santa doesn't bring everything kids ask for."

"But, Dave!" Laura protested. (My kids have always called their father Dave. They call me Mom, but only because I forced them to.) "A rat is the *only* thing I asked for!"

Laura did get her rat on Christmas morning. He was black and white. Laura decided he was a girl, even though that was obviously not true. Gradually, though, she came to accept the fact that he was a boy, and she named him Blaze. In kindergarten, the kids were asked to make trees out of construction paper, with red apples on which they had written the names of everyone in their family. Laura made apples for Laura, John, Mom, Dave, and Blaze. And she put Blaze's apple at the top of the tree.

We always put Blaze in our empty first-floor bathtub while we cleaned his cage. When John was about two and a half, he stole quietly into the bathroom while I wasn't looking. He closed the door and turned on the bathtub faucet, just to see what would happen. I heard the water running and ran to the bathroom. When I opened the door, I didn't have to say anything—John went immediately to time-out. But Blaze was fine.

Blaze was followed by a female rat named Brambles. I'm ashamed to say that I remember almost nothing about her—nice name, though!—except that we were worried she was lonely. A couple of weeks after we'd bought Brambles, we bought Tipsy. There was something the matter with Tipsy's sense of balance. She always held her head way over on one side and walked with her body kind of twisted over. She wasn't sick though. I thought maybe she'd had an injury or an infection when she was younger, but it had only affected her looks. And we knew Brambles wouldn't care about *that*.

We bought a second female rat because we didn't want millions of baby rats. But a week after she came to live here, Tipsy was much fatter. "Oh, well," I thought, "she's just bulking up." A week after that, she looked as if she had swallowed an apple whole. At that point I couldn't ignore what was going on. Rats can get pregnant when they're only five weeks old, so "something" must have happened at the pet store. Tipsy had been a few days pregnant when she came to live with us; now she was *very* pregnant.

Actually, this made me happy. I hadn't *planned* things this way, so no one could blame me. And we were going to have a new batch of babies in the house!

A rat's gestation period—the length of time she's pregnant—is about three weeks. Unfortunately, three and a half weeks after buying Tipsy, our family was due to go to Disneyland. As always, some pet crisis was getting in the way of our vacation, even though this wasn't a real crisis. We were sad that for a whole week we wouldn't be able to watch the babies.

On the other hand, the first week of a rodent's life isn't all that interesting. Baby rats, mice, and hamsters are just little pink eraser-looking things with no fur.

"Pinkies," they're called. The mother usually keeps the babies covered up, and she doesn't like people poking around the nest. In fact, she may even *eat* the babies if you bother them too much. My kids and I weren't great at leaving babies alone, so we knew it was for the best that we wouldn't be around that first week. But then Tipsy started having her babies the morning we were leaving, so we were able to see at least three pinkies in the nest before we took off. Would they still be alive when we came home? Would there be more of them?

I left a note for the friend who'd be taking care of the pets while we were away. "Give Tipsy lots of food and water," I wrote. A nursing mother needs to eat and drink way more than usual. "Keep the cage covered with a towel, and try not to peek in more than you have to," I went on. My friend had kids of her own, and I knew they would *have* to look at the babies once or twice.

TRIUMPHANT RETURN

Disneyland is a pretty good distraction. We didn't think much about the rats while we were away. But the minute we were back in the house, we all rushed over to Tipsy's cage.

Lying next to her was a huge pile of baby rats. All of them were nursing—well, almost all. A couple of them

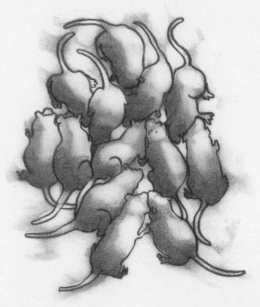

were squirmingly climbing over their pile of brothers and sisters, trying to get to nurse. Tipsy couldn't feed all the babies at once, because there were *THIRTEEN* of them.

"They look as though they're wearing little shirts!" said Laura, delighted. She was right. The babies' fur was still more like fuzz than fur—tightly fitting fuzz that was black and white, tan (we thought of it as golden), and spotted. Their eyes were still closed, and their tails were teeny instead of long and ratlike. Best of all, they had little snub snouts instead of long, pointed, ratty noses.

What they really looked like was tiny Labrador retriever puppies. Maybe that's why baby rats are called both ratlings and pups. All of us preferred "pups," and that's what we called the babies from then on.

They acted like puppies, too. We moved Tipsy's cage onto our kitchen table so that we could watch the babies as much as possible. This horrified a friend of ours who's a doctor, but I don't know why he was so upset. We also had a big cage of prairie dogs and two big birdcages in the kitchen. They were *much* messier than the rats, who were in a big glass tank. Anyway, even if the rat pups had spread deadly germs, which they didn't, it would have been worth it to watch them play. They wrestled and played hide-and-seek. They scrambled up onto the coffee can we had put into the tank and then jumped onto one another's backs. They grabbed bits of food from one another and scampered away with it. They really were exactly like little dogs.

The thing was, they didn't stay little for long. Pretty soon their noses got longer and pointier and their tails turned into true rat tails. Once they stopped nursing and started eating real food, their tank needed to be cleaned every minute, it seemed like. It was time to separate the boys from the girls—and time to find new homes for at least some of the babies.

I brought the rats to Sunday school for a visit, and

one or two were adopted by kids in my class. I also took the babies to the library on a crowded Saturday and found homes for a couple more of them that way. Whenever a crowd gathers around a bunch of baby animals, you can count on at least one kid being able to convince her mother that the family absolutely *has to have* one of the babies.

This is a small town, though, and we couldn't find homes for five of the females. So we kept them. "Okay, Brambles," I said. "I don't want to hear you complaining about being lonely ever again."

But a glass tank doesn't work as a home for seven rats. We bought a big two-story ferret cage like the one our sugar gliders and prairie dogs lived in, and we put it next to the prairie dogs' cage in the kitchen. The girls—as we called them now—weren't quite as fun to watch as when they'd been pups, but they were still entertaining. Unlike a hamster or a guinea pig, a rat never objects to being taken out of her cage. She's up for anything. If John and a friend wanted to make a block maze and put the rats in it, the girls were happy to oblige.

Once, a tremendously loud airplane flew over the house. All seven rats threw themselves to the bottom of their cage and flattened down, motionless.

When Tipsy died, two of her daughters buried her

under some newspaper. Then they sat on the newspaper. I'm still wondering what they meant by that.

Maybe that's not the right note to end on. It doesn't exactly prove why rats make such great pets. But I'm leaving it in, because I think it's cool.

If it bothers you, just cross it out.

Unless this is a library book.

Anyway, my point is this: put down this book and go get yourself a pet rat!

NAMES

Recently, a boy I know named Sam said to his dad, "I'd love to have my own pet shop. But you know what would be the hardest part? Coming up with a name for each pet."

Actually, of course, most pet-store owners don't bother naming the animals they're going to sell. But I know what Sam meant. It's a challenge to think up the perfect name for an animal.

Come to think of it, it's a challenge to think up the perfect name for a person. When Laura was born and the nurses in the hospital asked what we were going to name her, I wanted to say, "That's not up to *me,* is it?" It just seemed like such a huge responsibility to give a baby a name she would have for her *whole life!*

Especially because your idea of the perfect name can change so often. When I was little, some friends of my parents had a dog named Matilda. I thought that was the most beautiful, poetic name I had ever heard. I kept suggesting to my parents that they name their next baby Matilda if she turned out to be a girl. The next baby turned out to be a boy. By then I had decided that Christabelle was the most beautiful, poetic name I had ever heard, but my parents didn't have any more children after my brother. Not that they would have listened to me anyway. People like to come up with their own names for their kids.

That's one of the reasons having a lot of pets is fun: it gives you the chance to come up with a lot of names. When my husband was little, the only reason he *wanted* pets was so he could name them.

Since I've bought most of the pets in our house, I get to pick their names. Of course, my kids have always been allowed to name any pet that belonged to them. Laura named her first hamster Mary. She had gotten her as a Christmas present and wanted a Christmas-y name.

"Are you going to let her name a hamster Mary?" my sister asked.

"Sure!" I said. "You named *your* Christmas hamster Noel when we were little." Then I reminded her that our other sister had once named a doll Jesus.

By the way, Laura continued to have religious thoughts about Mary the hamster. When Mary died and I told Laura she was in heaven, Laura grumpily said, "I wish she weren't *His* pet."

Laura liked to call Mary "my pet" instead of "Mary" or even "my hamster." Once, a preschool friend of hers was coming over to play, and Laura said, "I do not want him to touch my white pet." Which was doubly odd, because Mary wasn't white. She was *tan* and white.

John once named some gerbils Fire Engine and Ambulance, those being his favorite vehicles at the time.

The important animals in our family I want to name myself, because I'm selfish and bossy. I named both our dogs, for instance. I just decided what their names would be and announced my decision to everyone. One reason for this: I didn't want my kids to name the dogs based solely on what they looked like. Children often do that—well, so do grownups, I guess. When she was little, Laura named one of our cats Creamsicle because he was orange and white. I loved Creamy, but I was always a bit embarrassed to tell people his name. It seemed so . . . obvious. The vet's office misspelled it "Creamsycle," as if he were some kind of bike. I would almost have preferred that.

On the other hand, I *love* it when kids name their pets by adding a *y* or an *ie* to the end of whatever kind of animal it is. "Hedgie," for example. My sister had a toy cat named Catty, and I had a toy Dalmatian named Dalmatiany. Laura had a toy seagull named Seag-y and a toy guinea pig named Guinea-y. (Meanwhile, John had a toy frilled lizard named Mint. John always goes against the tide.) We've borrowed this trick for many of the wild animals who live with us temporarily. When we thought one of our baby snapping turtles was going to die, we renamed him Dyingy and the other one Livingy. (Dyingy didn't die; we let him go near the pond where he had been found. We changed Livingy's name to Snappingy.)

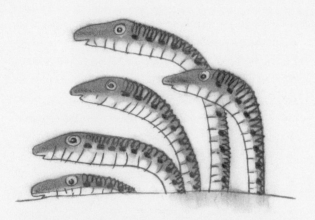

And when five baby garter snakes lived in a hole at the edge of our swimming pool, David named them Snakey, Snakey, Snakey, Snakey, and Snakey.

We always referred to the Snakeys as a single snake. "Did Snakey come out to see you?" I would ask David after his swim. The baby snakes did seem to like to watch him and would sometimes poke their heads out of the hole when he swam to that end of the pool.

"Today there were only three Snakeys," David might answer. He says that if he ever writes an autobiography, its title will be *And Their Name Was Snakey.*

I also love giving animals "people" names. We once had a baby robin named Jeff and another named Mary. For some reason, some members of my family don't like it when we name pets Mary.

"That's a ridiculous name for a robin," my father said to me.

"Who cares? *She* doesn't."

"And that's another thing," said my dad. "Why do you call her a girl?"

I'll tell you why. Because people always assume that if they don't know what sex an animal is, it must be a boy. (My husband's family took the idea even further, believing that all cats were girls and all dogs were boys. "Everyone believes this," my husband still says.)

In this book, I haven't bothered explaining how most of our pets got their names. It seems too boring to say things like "We named the baby owl Pecky because of his sharp-pecking beak." Except in one or two cases, here's how our pets got their names: I named them; the kids named them; we all named them, after a bunch of stupid arguing; or they came already named.

Or we didn't name them. Kids who visit are always shocked that I haven't named my pygmy mice. But how can you name twenty-six mice that look identical?

On the other hand, once I found out that my kids had actually named two of their sweatshirts. One was Gray-y, and one was Navy-y.

Now, that's just crazy.

make way for ducklings

Ducks do not belong inside a house.

Most people probably know this already. But it took me six ducklings' worth of training before I learned it myself.

The summer before Laura went into eighth grade, her friend Stephanie asked if we could take care of her ducklings for a couple of weeks while her family was in Scotland. Stephanie loves animals. As a little girl, she saw a skunk in the yard while she was out on her family's deck. Her mother told her to come inside quickly. Instead, Stephanie dropped a big box over the skunk, hoping to get a chance to look at it more closely. I don't remember what happened next.

Of course I said yes to the ducklings. We didn't have a big farm and a pond, as Stephanie's family did. Nor did we have a pen where the ducks could be locked up at night to keep them safe. But I was sure that a wading pool out on the screened porch would work fine. A door from the kitchen opens right out to the porch, so it would be easy to keep track of the babies. We could let them into the yard for exercise. "They'll come back when you call them to eat," Stephanie promised. Plus, she would leave her incubator containing two duck eggs that were just about to hatch. It would all be so educational!

And it *was* educational. The incubator, especially. When the ducklings were about to hatch, we could actually hear them peeping and pecking inside the eggs. A day later, we could see tiny pinpoint holes around the "waists" of the eggshells.

"Let's help the ducks by peeling the shells away!" the kids said. I said no, we had to be patient. That sounds just like what a mom would say, I know—but actually, baby birds *need* time to hatch on their own. They're still developing while they work to hatch. If you take them out of the shell before they're ready, they may die.

Even so, hatching is a chore. When the ducklings finally began to push their way out of their shells, they were damp and exhausted. They had to keep taking breaks. They'd lie there panting, half in and half out of the shells. Then they'd gather their strength and start struggling again. The job looked as hard for them as breaking through a concrete wall would be for us. But the next day, when they had perked up and fluffed out and were swimming around in a dishpan, they were perfect.

HOWEVER, THE REST OF
THE DUCKLINGS . . .

The incubator was the only easy part. The first day the rest of Stephanie's ducks were in our porch, they were pretty quiet—probably scared of their new surroundings. Once they had settled down, the ducklings started making noise. This is the sound they made all day long:

BEE BEE BEE BEE BEE BEE BEE BEE BEE
BEE BEE BEE BEE BEE BEE BEE BEE BEE
BEE BEE BEE BEE BEE BEE BEE BEE BEE
BEE BEE BEE BEE BEE BEE BEE BEE BEE
BEE BEE BEE BEE BEE BEE BEE BEE BEE
BEE BEE BEE BEE BEE BEE BEE BEE BEE!

All. Day. Long.

At least that was the sound they made when no one was nearby. If they heard footsteps, the sound would change to:

BEE BEE BEE BEE BEE BEE BEE
BEE BEE BEE BEE BEE BEE BEE
BEE BEE BEE BEE BEE BEE BEE
BEE BEE BEE BEE BEE BEE BEE
BEE BEE BEE BEE BEE BEE BEE

BEE BEE BEE BEE BEE BEE BEE BEE BEE BEE BEE BEE BEE BEE!

Beanie added to the noise by endlessly whining and crying and scratching at the porch door. He *lived* for seeing those ducks close up.

"My goodness, Beanie," I said sternly. "If I were to let you in there, I promise you'd be sick of the ducklings in no time." He didn't seem to care.

Our cats, of course, were even more interested in the ducklings. They surrounded the porch from the outside and endlessly watched Duckling TV, waiting for one of the babies to make a mistake. Whenever we let the ducklings out into the yard—which we were supposed to do twice a day—I had to fend off the cats with a broom.

Letting the ducks out was a problem in general. There was nothing more fun than watching them pad around the grass, trying to uproot bugs and worms with their tiny bright orange bills. And for a couple of days they did come when we called them. They'd rush back to the porch in a little line—waggling their rear ends, adorably hopping up the steps, and running up the slanted board that led to their wading pool.

After a few days, though, they discovered that there were even more bugs and worms *under* the porch. Then they weren't quite as eager to come inside for

some dry little pellets of food. One of the ducklings was a little older than the others—old enough that he had basically turned into a regular duck by the end of his visit. His wings were strong enough that he could almost fly, and he made a huge fuss when it was time to come in. We had to corner him and scoop him up, flapping and squawking and trying to peck our arms. This upset all the ducks, especially him.

And then of course these were ducks, not baby chicks—so they needed to be in water a lot of the time. In a pond, it doesn't matter when a duck poops, as long as you're not planning to swim right underneath. In a wading pool inside a porch, it *does* matter. There's so much poop, and it's so big, and the ducks are so good at producing it! And they won't stop splashing the poopy water around! Why, if all the ducklings are splashing at once, they may even manage to spray the *walls* with poopy water! You can certainly forget about keeping your feet and legs clean when you're in there.

Maybe the ducklings wouldn't have cared about swimming in filthy water, but *I* cared. Especially when they drank it. Laura, John, and I kept dragging the wading pool outside to drain it and refill it from the hose. Meanwhile, the cats—who had been waiting for this chance—would try to slither through the open door to get the ducks. Once, Creamsicle actually made it into the porch, and I got so mad that I sprayed him with the hose.

ALL ALONE, WITH DUCKS

The worst thing was that after ten days of our two-week Duck Prison, the rest of my family left to start our own vacation. I had been looking forward to some time alone before joining them, but now that I knew what I was in for, I felt very, very sorry for myself. Laura felt sorry for me, too. After all, Stephanie was *her* friend. She left me a bunch of little presents, one for each day I'd be on my own with the ducks. One was a duck-shaped pin, and one was a little pewter duck with a note that said, "This a lovely pewter duck, yah?" I still have them.

The minute my family's car pulled out of the driveway, I went into full crisis mode. *No way* was I going to let those ducks outside when I didn't have someone to help me get them back in again. From here on in, they would have to stay safe in the porch where I could keep an eye on them. I covered the whole porch floor, and all the furniture, with plastic sheets. (Meanwhile, the ducks were screaming BEE BEE BEE! and following me around.) Then I rushed to the store and bought a second wading pool. While the ducks were in one pool, I figured, I'd be able to clean out the other. This was supposed to cut down on my pool-cleaning time; instead, it doubled it. But at least it gave the ducks more water to exercise and poop in.

I wasn't home when Stephanie and her mom came to pick up all the babies. I can't imagine what the porch looked like when they finally got there, but remember the Greek myth where Hercules has to clean out the Augean stable? I bet it was a lot like that. Stephanie's mom told me later that she hadn't realized we didn't have a pond. "Ducks are livestock, not pets!" she told Stephanie. "They're not supposed to be inside."

By then, I had learned the same lesson. I'd rather keep a horse in my porch than any more ducklings.

But I wouldn't mind getting an incubator with a couple of duck eggs. Maybe when the ducks hatch, Stephanie can have them.

can you believe i ended up with all these cats?

When I was a preschooler, I wanted a kitten so badly that it was like a fever. We lived in an apartment complex then. When a kitten was born under a neighbor's sofa, I remember wondering if I could smuggle it into my own apartment. But I knew I'd never be able to pull it off, because my father was terribly allergic to cats. It was one of the main laws of my childhood: You Will Never, Ever Own a Cat. Parents are so unfair!

When I grew up, I married a man who was also allergic to cats. (A lot of people are.) David had actually grown up in a household where there was always a cat. "So you got used to them, right?" I asked hopefully. But no: he had stayed allergic to them. The rest of his family liked cats, so it was four to one and David lost.

Between David and my dad, though, I was stuck. There was, and is, no question of my ever having a cat in the house. And cats belong inside, so there was no way I'd ever have a cat. But by the time I was a grownup, I had persuaded myself that I didn't much want one anyway. Cats kill birds. They scratch. Their litter boxes are disgusting. They look mean. And so on. "I'm a dog person," I decided, and I stopped thinking about cats.

PERFECT, ADORABLE WHISKY

Then, when Laura was five and John was one and a half, Whisky wandered into our yard.

It was a wet fall afternoon, and Whisky was a sodden mass of long, drenched fur. Even his tail, which was as bushy as a raccoon's, streamed with rain. He stood outside the playroom window and looked in at us, meowing dejectedly.

"He's probably on his way home," I told the kids. I hoped it was true, though Whisky didn't look a bit like

a cat with a home. And he certainly wasn't "on his way" anywhere.

"How 'bout if we give him some food just to help him *get* home?" Laura asked.

I said no. "That would just make him hang around here, hoping for more food," I told her. It's what grownups always say in this situation, and it's true as far as it goes. The kids were used to hearing it—but not my friend Alex.

Alex and her husband, Bill, were visiting for the weekend. Alex has always had cats, and she couldn't stand seeing Whisky out there, crying. She didn't say anything, but a little later I saw her feeding Whisky on the porch, where he could be out of the rain. She had slipped out to the grocery store and bought a can of cat food for him.

Bill pulled Alex aside and whispered something to her. Something like "Alex, we can't break the rules of the house like this"—you know, something an adult *would* say. Alex bit her lip and didn't answer. She didn't look at all sorry, and I don't blame her. She had done the right thing.

The next morning, Whisky strolled back into the yard. By now it had stopped raining. His fur wasn't quite so awful, and he looked more cheerful. The kids ran out to greet him. He rolled over onto his back, purring, and let Laura pick him up and lug him around the yard. He also let her pull him along in her wagon. He let John pat him with the hard pats of an eighteen-month-old baby. Nothing seemed to bother him. He was more like a dog than any cat I'd ever seen.

Here's what I always say in these situations: "I had no choice, did I?"

"I won't let him in the house," I promised David. "I'll just feed him outside for a couple of days. We'll see what happens."

What happened was that in a few days, David said, "There couldn't be a nicer cat. Maybe you should take him in to get vaccinated and neutered." A couple of weeks after that, David built Whisky a nice little house with a shingled roof. (David was teaching himself how to shingle at the time, so this was good practice.) He lined it with sweaters and old towels. Whisky walked inside the minute David set it down on the back step, and he stayed with us for ten happy years.

GRUMPY, GRUMPY CREAMSICLE

Is there some way stray cats send a message to other strays? Something to let them know "the people here will feed you"? Or is our neighborhood full of homeless cats who make the rounds of all the houses at night, looking for food? Whatever the case, Creamsicle moved into our yard a few months after Whisky had joined the family.

We first knew Creamsicle was there when I heard a weird yodel coming from the patio. I looked out to see a scrawny orange and white cat pacing back and forth, staring at Whisky and uttering a sort of wavering yowl. Whisky watched him calmly. Nothing upset Whisky. This was a cat, after all, who let the kids carry him around in a snow shovel. Besides, Creamsicle had no excuse for being grouchy. It wasn't *his* yard, and there was plenty of food for both cats. As soon as Creamsicle started eating out of Whisky's dish, I gave him his own dish. I had no choice, did I? We couldn't let Whisky worry that he'd have to share his food.

In any case, Creamsicle and Whisky soon came to love each other. They crammed together into Whisky's

little house and slept with their arms around each other. One was never far from the other for as long as Whisky was alive, and after Whisky died, Creamsicle walked around, hunting for him and crying for several days.

Whisky was the *only* thing that made Creamsicle happy. We soon discovered that Creamsicle's main pleasure in life was complaining. If the dogs didn't come up and rub noses with him, he complained. If it was hot, he complained. If it was cold, he complained. If he saw us through the screen door, he complained. He'd park himself outside the front door and stare at it, moaning sorrowfully every few seconds. All you could see through the screen was his ears. The ears of sorrow, I called them.

Creamsicle's complaints were so predictable—he moaned when you said *anything* to him—that we invented a kind of conversation with him. It consisted of giving him bad news, to which he would make a sad reply. Like this:

"Creamy, I just heard the worst thing."

"Mreoowwwwwwwoooooo . . ." Creamsicle would quaver.

"Queen Victoria's dead!"

"Mreoowwwwwwwoooooo . . ."

"Plus, an earthquake destroyed the whole world!"

"Mreoowwwwwwwoooooo . . ."

"Do you have any comments?"

"Mreooooooowwwwoooooooo . . ."

"I agree with you. It's a tragedy."

It makes me so sad to write about Creamsicle's sad end. I only want to describe the happy times with my cats in this chapter. So I've told the rest of Creamsicle's story a little later. (Jimmy, another very important cat, is in another chapter as well.) For now I'm going to move on to Todd.

BAD KITTY/TODD THE INVADER

One morning Whisky and Creamsicle were eating breakfast when a huge gray tom strode onto the front porch and pushed them out of the way. He really did. He shouldered his way between them, and they kind of melted out of sight. Calmly, the big cat finished their food. Then he strolled away, licking his whiskers.

"What a *bad kitty*," I said soothingly to Whisky and Creamsicle. "Don't worry. He won't be coming back."

But Bad Kitty kept showing up. "Have you seen that huge gray cat?" one of my neighbors asked. "He keeps looking through my windows and terrorizing Fiona." Fiona was her Persian, who never went outside except on a leash.

"Mommy! There's a panther in the yard!" Laura gasped one evening when she saw Bad Kitty stalking along.

Bad Kitty terrorized *my* cats, too. He was so powerful it seemed almost supernatural. I once saw him jump straight into the air, like a basketball player, and *bat* a bird off my birdfeeder. (After that, I stopped putting out birdseed. No reason to turn birds into cat bait.) If he took a step toward Whisky or Creamsicle, they'd back off, yowling low in their throats; then, when they were at a safe distance, they'd streak away.

And yet Bad Kitty was very nice to *us*. You could tell he had once belonged to someone. He had been neutered, and he clearly thought he had a right to come inside our house. In fact, he once snuck in and spent the night pacing around our first floor.

After a couple of months, Bad Kitty could still be found hanging around the yard, and my cats were still miserable. Although I could hardly believe I was doing something so dopey, I decided to visit a cat psychologist and see if she could help us.

She might have been even more helpful if she'd been able to meet Bad Kitty, but that didn't work out. On the morning of his appointment, I couldn't find him anywhere. (This always seems to happen when you have an outdoor cat whom you need to put into a cat carrier.) So I just went by myself and described the problem to her.

"Bad Kitty sounds as though he *has* to dominate the other two cats," the psychologist said. "He's bigger than they are, and stronger than they are, and he's not going to give up until they accept that. You'll just have to wait it out until they establish a pecking order. Cats usually work things out on their own."

It was discouraging. I had hoped she would be able to teach me some magical hypnosis techniques that would turn Bad Kitty into a sweet puffball. Either that, or I'd hoped she would tell me how to make Whisky and Creamsicle stand up to him. I wanted *them* at the top of the pecking order, not Bad Kitty! "Wait it out" is just the kind of advice I hate.

The cat psychologist was right, though. Very, very gradually, things calmed down among the three cats. I would feed Whisky and Creamsicle at the front door and Bad Kitty at the back door. True, when he was done eating he would stroll jauntily around to the front to see if he could get any of their food. True, if either of them came close to him, Bad Kitty would suddenly dart at them and chase them away. But at least all three cats were carving out their own territories.

I've always been surprised to see how eagerly cats will tell you when something is wrong with them. Since my cats live outside, I'd expect them just to wander into the woods and suffer when they're not feeling well. Yet they mostly come and show me or David that something is the matter. Maybe they don't realize that this will result in our taking them to the vet. Or maybe they do! In any case, one afternoon Bad Kitty limped up to me, meowing plaintively. He held out his front paw, which was so swollen that it looked like a baseball glove.

"It's an abscess," the vet said an hour later. "It will need to be drained and he'll need stitches."

"Why don't you give him all his vaccinations while you're at it?" I asked. "I guess he really is our cat now."

I told the vet's receptionist that his name was Bad Kitty.

Bad Kitty came through the surgery fine, but as soon as we got him home he took off. We didn't see him again for almost a week. Then a note in an unfamiliar handwriting showed up in our mailbox.

"I want to thank you for taking care of Todd's abscess," the note said. "I was so worried when I didn't see him for five days—but he always comes home. When I saw the stitches, I called all the vets in the area to find out who had helped him. Thank you for your loving kindness, neighbor."

Neighbor? Yes. *Next-door* neighbor, as it turned out. (Her house was far enough away that we hadn't met.) Todd, our "Bad Kitty," was her cat—one of five. All the time that I had been worrying about helping Todd to get along with my cats, he'd had a home of his own right next door. A house he could go inside to keep warm, if he wanted to, and a place where there was plenty of food. He just *liked* hanging around my yard.

For the next couple of years, my neighbor and I shared Todd. Then her husband got a job in another state, and the family moved away. "Wouldn't you like to keep Toddy?" she asked. "He loves being with you."

So Todd became our third cat. And I would say he is our busiest cat, too. He has assigned himself many chores around the yard. The main one is "helping" me whenever I take the garbage cans down to the end of the driveway for the garbage collector. Todd always *rushes* to walk along next to me. He stands on the stone wall as if he's supervising the placement of each garbage can. He trots alongside as I return to the garage to get the next can and jumps up onto the wall to make sure I'm doing everything right. When the job is done, he rolls over so I can pat his stomach.

After our neighbors moved, I called the vet's office to say that we'd be in charge of Todd from then on. "You should change his name on the file," I said. "He's not Bad Kitty anymore."

"I never liked that name anyway," said the vet's receptionist. "I wrote him down as *Good* Kitty."

And he really is a very good kitty.

GRAYDON AND HIS PROBLEMS

After we'd found out what Todd's real name was, we used the name Bad Kitty for any cat who wandered into the yard and tried to join our cat club. Most of these new Bad Kitties ended up leaving. I suspect that many of them had homes and were just stopping at our place for a snack. One Bad Kitty who was even bigger than Todd hung around for a few months, but it turned out that he, too, belonged to our next-door neighbors. His real name was Stripe, and when they moved they took Stripe with them. Then we adopted Jimmy from a shelter, and for a while it looked as though we were done getting new cats.

To tell you the truth, I don't remember how Graydon came into our lives. He seems always to have been here. I know that when we first noticed him, he looked completely different from the rest of the cats. His short, stiff fur was pure gray—no faint stripes or dots the way most housecats have—and he didn't have a fluffy undercoat like the rest of the cats. It wasn't the nicest coat I've ever seen on a cat—kind of skimpy—but you couldn't help noticing the color. It was the kind of gray that cat breeders call blue.

Actually, Graydon was kind of skimpy all over. His legs were skinny and bent, and so was his tail. And even more than Creamsicle, he complained. Like Todd, he thought he had a right to come inside our house. Unlike Todd—who would cheerfully walk away when we shoved him back outside—he would stay right by the door, peering and yowling and waiting for another chance to sneak in. And if you shoved him outside too vigorously, he would have an asthma attack.

That's what really separated Graydon from our other cats— his asthma. He had the first serious attack soon after we started taking care of him. I found him leaning against the side of the house, his eyes rolled back in his head. His mouth was lolling open as he tried to suck in air. His chest was shuddering up and down. I had never seen an animal with asthma, and I was scared. I rushed Graydon to the vet's office. He hated being in the cat carrier and had diarrhea on the way. This caused me to speed up even more. In fact, I went so fast that a policeman stopped me, and then drove behind me until I got to the vet's. He didn't give me a ticket when he smelled my car. "Just be careful going home," he said.

What can it be like for my cats? They come into our yard and find a pleasant place to settle down. There's plenty of food and a choice of cat houses to sleep in if it gets too cold. And then, as soon as they're tame enough, I grab them, pop them into a cat carrier, and take them to the vet to be neutered and vaccinated. What a welcome! I'm amazed they stick around the yard after that.

But Graydon was lucky to meet our vet, because all he needed was a couple of shots to get him back in shape. Now he takes a pill every day for his asthma. (I hide the pill in a pellet made of cream cheese.) It makes his breathing easier, though I don't think he'll ever be completely comfortable. His chest heaves way too much when he breathes, and he can't purr. Maybe that's why he's so complain-y.

The strange thing about Graydon is that although

he's so puny, he's the *total* boss of all the other cats—including Todd. How is this possible? He was the last to arrive, and he's by far the weakest. Todd could knock him over with his tail! And yet if Graydon walks up to Todd or Jimmy and even *sniffs* them, they back away. Sometimes one of the other cats will be eating and won't notice when Graydon sneaks up. Graydon sits there awhile and watches. Then he leans out a front paw and pokes the other cat with it. The other cat always dashes off, and Graydon strolls over for any leftover food.

Graydon has even attacked raccoons who are twice his size. At night, the neighborhood raccoons always make the rounds of our cat dishes. Todd and Jimmy sit back and watch meekly. Graydon perches on the edge of the steps and waits. When a raccoon waddles up to the dishes, Graydon *hurls* himself down onto its back and rides it for a few steps while it escapes. Then he hops off and comes back to the steps.

There's some kind of lesson here, but I don't know what it is. If you're the weakest, cheer up because you can still be a bully? That doesn't sound right.

Graydon is also the most curious of our cats. If we're shoveling snow, Graydon stands in front of us to supervise every shovelful. (Complaining, of course. "Why can't you shovel away *all* the snow?" he's probably saying.) When I get groceries out of the car, Graydon trots up to see what I've bought. When I cut the dogs' toenails outside on the patio, Graydon shoves up under my arm to see why they're so upset.

Oh, and that reminds me of the main thing about Graydon: He thinks he *is* a dog. He has no interest in making friends with the other cats, but when he sees Moxie and Beanie, he rubs them all over with his head. Whenever we take the real dogs out, Graydon parks himself next to them and squats down to pee, too. Cats are usually quite private about bathroom stuff, but not Graydon. You can tell he's thinking, "This is the way we dogs like to do it. Pretty soon those humans will let me into their house along with the other dogs."

I think I have enough cats. The thing is, though, that we live in a place where a lot of barn cats always need homes. A couple of weeks ago I was visiting a farm where there were four identical black barn kittens. Barn cats are sometimes shy, but these kittens followed me all over the place, leaping and rolling and pouncing on my feet whenever I stopped walking.

"They're free to a good home," the farmer who owns the barn said hopefully.

I've always wanted a kitten. The problem is that most kittens can't live outside. But these kittens *already* live outside.

I wonder what will happen next.

the worst day

I've already told you how complain-y Creamsicle was. But Creamsicle was braver than any animal should have to be whenever he was hurt or sick. He was in and out of the vet's a lot with abscesses, infected toes, and the leftover wounds from fights with other cats. He got a lot of his injuries from wandering through the woods around our house. He wouldn't drink from a water bowl; he only liked "wild water" from puddles or the creek across the street. He also liked to prowl around through the big drainage pipe on our hill and would camp out there in a rainstorm. Sometimes he'd be gone for a day or two, and as he got older and his fur got thinner, I started worrying about him more and more. But he was always home by breakfast time.

Creamy loved to sit in front of one of the windows that look down into our basement. There he could keep warm while he watched me feeding the indoor pets—and there, of course, he could complain to me. "You should really let me inside," he'd say. "I'm *just* as nice as those stupid birds and rabbits. I'd be no trouble down in the basement. The poor, shabby basement's a fine place for an old wreck like me."

He really was getting old. We had never known his exact age, but the vet figured he had to have been at least two or three when he first wandered into our yard, and ten years had passed since then. One year, David and I were sure he wouldn't last through the winter. I thought about finding him an indoor home, but as long as he stayed in his little wooden house (which was well insulated), he was warm enough. And cats hate change, especially older cats; I was sure Creamsicle would miss complaining to us. He made it through that winter, and through the next one. "He's tougher than we think," I kept saying.

THE ACCIDENT

One bitterly cold January day—the third winter after Creamsicle had started to seem ancient—I was feeding the bulbul when a shadow fell across the basement window. I looked up—and took a step back. What *was* that silent shape? It looked like a cat, but what kind of cat?

It took several seconds before I realized that I was

looking at Creamsicle. His face was so smashed up that I hadn't recognized him.

My heart was pounding so hard I felt sick. I ran upstairs and outside. Creamsicle was huddled up against the window, covered with blood and dirt. When he heard my voice, he let out a dreadful wail.

He had been attacked by some kind of animal, and it had bitten him from the top of his head through to his chin. His face was now shaped like the blade of an axe—flat and smooth, with no curving forehead and no nice little cat muzzle. I couldn't see his eyes; the top of his skull had slid down to cover them completely. There was a crushed indentation where the bridge of his nose should have been.

Somehow Creamsicle had managed to drag himself back to his usual window, hoping I would notice him.

There was no time to get upset. I rushed back inside to get the cat carrier and a pair of rubber gloves. As in so many places, rabies is a threat where I live. All my pets are up to date on their rabies vaccinations; the danger this time was to me. If Creamsicle's attacker had been rabid, and if any of its saliva was still on Cream-sicle's fur, I didn't want to come into contact with it.

Creamsicle didn't protest when I put him into the cat carrier. He crumpled like a folding chair and lay limp and silent all the way to the vet's. Usually it makes me frantic when my cats yowl in the car, but that day I realized how lucky I am that they feel well enough to complain. Having grouchy old Creamsicle be so quiet was much worse.

"Well, it wasn't a coyote. I think a woodchuck bit him," said the vet, Dr. Ferris, a few minutes later.

"A *woodchuck*?" I asked. "A woodchuck would attack a cat?"

"It would if Creamsicle came into its burrow. And its teeth would be strong enough to bite through his skull like this."

It sounded all too possible. I knew how much Creamy liked to explore pipes and drains. What if he'd discovered a woodchuck tunnel and poked his head inside?

Creamsicle might also have been attacked by a fisher cat. Despite their name, fisher cats are actually members of the weasel family. They're much bigger and stronger than weasels, though, and are fiercely aggressive; they'll even eat porcupines. There aren't many fisher cats in the woods around my house. I've never seen one myself. But fishers have attacked several pets in my neighborhood over the past few years.

Of course, it didn't matter what kind of animal had done this to Creamsicle.

"I know you can't do anything for him," I said in a trembling voice. "You'll have to put him to sleep, right?"

But Dr. Ferris paused. "Creamsicle's pretty tough," he said. "He's managed to survive a lot. Leave him here and let me see what I can do." Then he looked down at the table. "Is he *purring*?" he asked.

He was. Lying on the vet's table on a bloody towel, Creamsicle had suddenly begun to purr and knead his paws. Sometimes cats purr when they're frightened or sick, but Dr. Ferris and I both believed Creamsicle was telling us he was happy to be in a safe place.

THE RACCOON

I had thought that day couldn't get any worse. But when I arrived home from the vet's, a raccoon with rabies was walking around in my yard.

Whenever you see a wild mammal in the daytime, it's a bad sign. Deer, mice, and squirrels are just about the only exceptions to this rule. Most wild mammals are nocturnal—active during the night instead of the day. Unless they're very young or very, very hungry, they won't venture out in daylight. Especially not where people can see them. You should *never*, *ever* pat *any* wild animal, no matter how friendly it seems. But if a raccoon, fox, or skunk lets you get close to it, *you must get out of there.* Even if the animal doesn't look sick, you need to get away and call for help.

This raccoon looked very sick. He was taking small, shaky steps and falling over. I knew the possibility of

rabies was already in my mind because of what had happened to Creamsicle—but I also knew I wasn't imagining things here. I ran inside and called our town's state trooper.

Police in this area are used to getting emergency calls about rabid animals, and they always ask why you think the animal has rabies. When I described the raccoon's symptoms, the trooper said, "Stay inside until I get there."

My family and the dogs were already inside. I was afraid the raccoon might attack the cats who were still outside, but I knew they were up-to-date on their rabies vaccinations. I knew, too, that they would probably leave the raccoon alone. Anyway, I couldn't go outside to get them. I just had to wait.

In five minutes, I saw the trooper's car pull into the driveway. I opened the back door and pointed to the raccoon, but the trooper had already seen him. He jumped out of his car, pistol in hand, and shot the raccoon through the head.

This wasn't like one of those Gentle Ben–type stories where a cruel person wants to shoot a wild animal just because he's gotten too big to live around people, or something like that. This was real life. Rabies is incurable. Rabid animals have to be killed. But that doesn't make it any easier to watch it happen.

"Okay, see you around," said the trooper. He opened his car door and started to get back in.

"What are you going to . . . what happens to the body?" I asked.

"You can just put it out with the garbage," he told me. "Wear gloves."

Hey, thanks! I wanted to say. *I could have figured that part out for myself!* But of course the trooper's part of the job was over.

By now it was afternoon on one of those winter days when it seems to get dark at four o'clock. I couldn't deal with the raccoon right then. Anyway, I didn't want to touch the body—even in gloves—while the blood was still fresh. I went to the garage and got a big, empty garbage can. Upending it over the raccoon's body, I went inside again. I would wait until the body was frozen solid before I dealt with it. Even though I hadn't touched the raccoon, I washed my hands for a long time. Then I took a shower.

Was there any chance that the raccoon had been Creamsicle's attacker? I called the vet, but he didn't think so. In any case, I'd been wearing gloves when I touched Creamsicle myself. The rabies virus dies quickly when it's exposed to the air. I hadn't touched the raccoon, and none of its blood had touched me. It was just a nasty coincidence at the end of an awful afternoon.

CREAMSICLE AT THE HOSPITAL

The next day I visited Creamsicle at the animal hospital. They were keeping him in a cage away from the other cats, at one end of the operating room. I wasn't allowed in there during operations, of course, so I came in when the day's surgeries were over.

I pulled up a stool and sat as close to the cage as I could, trying to keep out of the vets' way while they walked around. At first I was afraid to touch Creamsicle. He looked so sick. The infection from the wound smelled terrible. There was one drainage tube in his head to carry away blood and fluids from the bite, and another in his front paw to give him food and water. But he was being given plenty of painkillers, and he seemed glad to see me. I could feel him purring when I touched him. So even though I was crying, I tried to sound cheerful.

"You look just awful, Creamy," I said lightly. "What a wreck! But soon you'll be gorgeous again."

How could that be true? I wondered. And even if Creamsicle did recover, what was I going to do with him in the middle of winter? He certainly wouldn't be able to live outside now or ever. While I patted him, my mind kept going around and around. Maybe he'd be here for long enough that by the time he recovered it would be warm again. But that would mean keeping him imprisoned for weeks, away from everything he was used to. Maybe I could fix up a place in the house for him where he'd be far enough away that David's allergies wouldn't flare up. Or should I find another home for him somewhere? But who would adopt a cat this old and this badly hurt?

I visited Creamsicle every afternoon, and I worried about him pretty much all the time. The smell of his infection seemed always to be in my nose. Confusingly, Creamy seemed cheerful as the days went on. It got so I could pick him up and hold him on my lap. Of course, he didn't know how bad he looked. He would put his front feet on my shoulders and stand up to rub his awful face against mine just the way he'd always done.

But I knew he wasn't getting better. And I was afraid to say anything to Dr. Ferris, because I knew he knew it, too.

On the tenth day, the animal hospital was quiet enough that I was able to take Creamsicle into one of the examining rooms where we could be alone. I was sitting in a chair holding him when Dr. Ferris opened the door and looked in at me.

"We need to talk about Creamsicle," he said.

"I know," I said.

And he told me what I already knew. Creamsicle would never recover. Even with the help of a miracle, he would never be able to see again; the bones of his skull had slid down over his eyes. Even if he had been strong enough for surgery, his skull was too shattered to repair. He would never be able to eat on his own again.

They could keep him alive, but they couldn't heal him—which would only be cruel. I had to say good-bye to him. I decided to do it right away before I lost my nerve.

"Let's put him to sleep," I said.

"Do you want to stay with him?" asked Dr. Ferris.

Of course I did. We hadn't come all this way together to have me leave Creamsicle alone when he died.

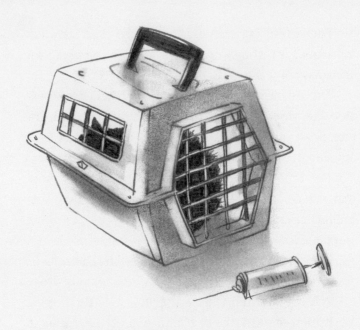

Here's what happens when an animal is put to sleep:

You get a few minutes alone with the animal to say your goodbyes.

The vet and a technician come into the examining room and put a towel down on the examining table. Gently they spread the pet out on the towel. You can see they hate having to do this. "It's okay," they tell the animal. "You're going to be all right."

If you can manage it, you join in these comforting words. After all, you don't want the animal to be more scared than it already is. It shouldn't hear the tears in your voice.

The technician puts a tight rubber strap called a tourniquet around the animal's leg. This makes the veins easier for the vet to find.

The vet fills a syringe with the medicine that will stop the animal's heart and injects the vein, and the technician undoes the tourniquet so the medicine can spread into the animal's bloodstream.

The animal breathes once or twice. Then, faster than you can imagine, the animal's body sags, limp and unbreathing, onto the table.

You can't believe it's over. The animal looks so relaxed and unchanged—exactly as if it's fallen asleep. You want to cry to the vet, "Stop! Wait! I changed my mind! Bring him back!"

You've seen for yourself how painless and easy it was. You know the animal won't suffer anymore and that this is for the best. But when the vet goes out and leaves you alone for a few minutes with your pet, you're still so shocked at how fast it was that you don't understand what's happening.

You pick up the pet—so floppy now—and stupidly try to explain to it what just happened. Your tears are falling onto its fur. You wish you could stay in the room, but you know they need the examining table for other people's animals. Besides, you remind yourself, your pet can't hear you anymore. Even though that's still impossible to believe.

So you leave the body on the table for them to send to be cremated. You'll get the ashes later.

Or you put the animal into its carrier to take home to bury.

If you give them the body, you keep wanting to say, "You guys won't let him get hurt, right?"

If you take the body home, you keep wanting to talk to it.

It won't make any sense for a long time.

SOME OF THE BEST THINGS
ABOUT PRAIRIE DOGS

For a long time I couldn't decide whether even to tell you about my prairie dogs.

Prairie dogs aren't legal for sale in the United States. There was a time when you could buy them, but then a few years ago people began to worry that they could spread diseases. I myself don't think this is a worry, but I do think that prairie dogs shouldn't be pets. *They need to dig,* and there's no way most people can give them the digging space they need. They need many, many companions, too. Prairie dogs are colony animals, and keeping them by themselves is a slow form of torture.

Besides, most of the baby prairie dogs that used to be for sale were wild-captured. They were vac-uumed out of their burrows by big machines, and then their mothers were killed and the babies were sold as pets. No animal lover can support that kind of business.

I know a woman who raises abandoned prairie dogs—abandoned by their human owners, I mean. In the days when it was legal to own prairie dogs as pets, many, many people got rid of them. They didn't have the patience to keep their prairie dogs happy, and they hadn't realized that a prairie dog can live for ten years. So, like selfish pet owners everywhere, they dumped them. This woman has forty rescued prairie dogs, and *hers* live the way they should—outside, in burrows they've dug for themselves. They can't escape, because she's buried a huge upside-down cage in the field where they live. (It's made of chain-link fencing.) But they can dig to their little diggy hearts' content.

Why shouldn't they escape? you may be wondering. Wouldn't they be better off free? No, no, no. This is the wrong part of the country for prairie dogs. They'd be killed by predators immediately, or they'd starve to death, or they'd be killed by people who didn't know they were tame. And supposing they did somehow manage to flourish, what would happen to the other burrowing mammals who live around here? Would there be enough food for all these species?

So anyway, it's better that prairie dogs can't be pets anymore.

On the other hand, my three prairie dog girls were some of my favorite pets ever. So I've decided to tell you about them after all—only I'm going to cheat a little. I'm just going to list some of the good things about my prairie dogs. Then my conscience will be (sort of) clear. I'll be paying tribute to darling Buttercup, Daisy, and Maisie, but I won't be writing an official *chapter* about them.

- Buttercup was the first prairie dog I got. She needed company—in the wild, prairie dogs are used to living in colonies of thousands and even hundreds of thousands—so a year after she'd come to live with us, we got Daisy to be her friend. Buttercup was round and solid by then, and baby Daisy looked like a skimpy little rat in comparison. But when we put Daisy into Buttercup's cage, the two girls put their paws on each other's shoulders and exchanged a long, tender sniff that was almost like a kiss.

- Prairie dogs really do make a kind of yipping sound, though it's not much like a bark. It's more like a high, shrill "*Wacka!*" The prairie dog will greet you with a wacka if she hears you coming into the house. If you startle her while she's sleeping, she'll let out a muffled "*Wacka!*"

- Once Daisy had also grown into a big, round, solid girl, the two prairie dogs looked like a pair of slippers when they slept next to each other.

- And speaking of sleeping, Buttercup and Daisy actually made their bed every night before they went to sleep. With lots of squeaks and clucks and bustling, they would fluff up their pile of towels, shredded paper, and hay. They would spread their bedding and try it out, then spread it again until it was just right. Finally they would climb in, pull the towels over themselves, and go to sleep until morning.

- Prairie dogs use hay, shoelaces, and pieces of string as dental floss. (True!) I used to tie shoelaces all over their cage so they could work on them. I would put some of the laces just out of reach so that the girls would have to climb to find them. When I let the prairie dogs out to play, they always rushed up to attack my own shoelaces.

- Prairie dogs love cut-up grapes as a treat. They stand to eat them, looking just like miniature people eating a wedge of watermelon.

- You have to keep a prairie dog *busy*. Really, really busy. My girls lived in a two-story ferret cage with a huge exercise wheel I bought from a prairie dog store out West. (Running on the wheel replaced some of their digging needs, even though their efforts never produced a tunnel.) For several years their cage was in our kitchen, next to some shelves that held cookbooks and folded cloth napkins. Once in a while, if the cage had been pushed close enough to the shelves, Buttercup and Daisy would help themselves to a napkin. They would pull it through the bars of their cage and then shred it to add to their pile of bedding.

After they had done this a few times, I got the idea of tying pieces of cloth to the outside of their cage for them to gradually pull inside. The bigger the piece of cloth, the harder they had to work to figure out how to get it through the bars of the cage. But there was no piece of cloth that they couldn't defeat in the end. They could have pulled a carpet into their cage if they'd had enough time.

- I liked to let Buttercup and Daisy out for exercise in my husband's and my bathroom. The girls would pad excitedly around, occasionally running back to touch my foot. I don't know why they did that. Maybe it reassured them in a strange place.

- Each prairie dog has its own personality. From the first minute we got her, Buttercup loved being held and patted. But she didn't like having

strangers put their fingers into her cage, and
sometimes she bit them. For a long time, Daisy
didn't like anyone touching her. (I have a scar on
my arm from when she bit me so hard that her
teeth met.) After Buttercup died, though, I was
sure that Daisy missed all the snuggling she'd
had with her friend.

"Whether you like it or not," I told her, "you're
going to have to get used to being patted." I put
on some leather gloves, opened the cage, and
gave Daisy some firm, strong pats on her head.
To my surprise, she snuggled right down under
my hand. After that, she let me pat her and take
her out of the cage all the time.

• With Buttercup gone, I knew Daisy now needed
a new friend. I found a breeder who had six
available prairie dogs and had him select the

friendliest one in the group. I decided I would name her Maisie.

Picking Maisie up from that breeder was one of the strangest experiences of my life. All the animals' cages were in a big room that it may have been an office at some point. There, they could be let out for exercise. A couple of large desert tortoises were slowly roaming the floor. In an adjoining room with a big glass window— maybe it had been a receptionist's office—there was a fennec running around and around and around and *around and around* in ceaseless, panting circles. "Wouldn't you like to buy the fennec, too?" asked the breeder. "I can't find anyone who wants him." But I said no. I could tell from its behavior that a fennec couldn't possibly be a good indoor pet, and by then I had learned that you shouldn't get an animal just because you feel sorry for it. Just because it doesn't have a good home doesn't mean *you* can give it a good home. (Of course, I've gotten all kinds of animals just because I felt sorry for them. Do as I say, not as I do!)

In a closet in one corner of the big room was a—"What *is* that?" I asked the breeder. It was a binturang that someone had abandoned; the breeder had given it a home. The binturang looked like a mixture of bear and cat. It had shaggy black fur and long arms. I guess the closet was a better place for it than a cage, but it was eerie to see the poor thing looking out of the door's barred window like a prisoner.

I see that this isn't one of the good things about a prairie dog. But the point is, Maisie came home with me that night and turned out to be the sweetest of all three girls.

- After Daisy died and Maisie was on her own, I thought about getting another prairie dog. But I couldn't warm up to the idea of extending the chain of misery that seems to be connected with prairie dog pups. Maybe I could have found a breeder who actually raised her own prairie dogs—but that would mean having the baby shipped to my house in an airplane. How scary that would be for the poor prairie dog!

And what would happen when Maisie died? Would I go on replacing prairie dogs forever? No, I decided. I wouldn't. Maisie would have to be the last of her kind at my house.

But oh, she was lonely. So lonely that I bought a secondhand Snugli on eBay so I could start carrying her around. If you have a baby brother or sister, you must have seen a Snugli. It's one of those baby carriers that you strap on to your chest so you can hold a baby without using your hands.

Of course, a human baby can't wriggle out through the Snugli's leg holes the way Maisie can. She loves being carried, but she doesn't like to stay put. Before I fixed the Snugli, I might be reaching up to get some birdseed for my finches when I would suddenly feel Maisie clawing her way out and grabbing onto my knee. After a few adventures like this, I sewed the leg holes shut. Now Maisie cuddles down with only her head peeking out while I do my chores.

I mean, she *usually* snuggles down. Sometimes she'll suddenly scramble *up* out of the Snugli and try to climb me like a tree. But that's what makes a Snugli so great: it leaves your hands free so you can grab your prairie dog and stuff her back into the pocket.

You sure can't do that with a human baby.

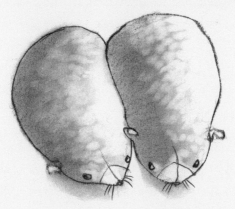

all my vets

On one wall of my living room is a big mural painted by an artist we know. It shows an imaginary landscape dotted here and there with buildings that are important to us. Our house is there, of course, and lots of our friends' houses. The artist didn't place them in their actual locations. She just put them wherever they'd look nicest. Two of the buildings are from other parts of the country: our summer place on Martha's Vineyard and the Augusta National Golf Club, which my husband once wrote a book about. My church is there, too.

When visitors see the painting for the first time, they just think it's a landscape. Then, maybe, they recognize our house and a couple of other places. After a minute or so, they realize what the artist has done. But they always have one question: "What's that big house in the foreground?"

The biggest building in the painting, the one in front of our house, is our vet's office. The artist figured that

since so many animals were part of our family, we probably went to the vet's more often than anywhere else.

We certainly see veterinarians more often than we see *people* doctors. Beanie, Moxie, and the cats all need checkups once a year. I can bring the dogs to the same appointment, but the cats have to come one at a time because—well—I can usually only *find* one cat at a time. (Even if I hide the cat carrier, the cats always seem to know that it's nearby.) The cats and dogs all need various vaccinations or a booster shot at least once a year. Whenever we go on vacation, the dogs stay at the vet's boarding kennel; if we're away in cold weather, the cats board there as well. Meanwhile, someone who works at the vet's office comes to the house twice a day to take care of our other animals.

And then there are all the various little problems each dog and cat may have. Both dogs have bad backs. One of the cats has asthma; another gets abscesses on his feet a lot. One dog and one cat have allergies. And so on. Over the course of the year, we probably go to the regular vet's office seven or eight times.

Our regular vets are a father-and-son team. Everyone calls them Dr. Ferris and Dr. Mike. They both live in our town, and both play golf with my husband. Another golfing friend of theirs, who hates to go to people doctors, always goes to Dr. Ferris for his checkups. His wife is listed on his medical chart as his "owner."

If there had been space in our living-room mural, the artist could have added the many other vets' offices I've used over the years. Dr. Ferris and Dr. Mike don't usually treat exotic animals, although I've brought them some of my other pets in emergencies. (I once brought in a pygmy mouse whose tail had been bitten. Dr. Ferris told me just to leave the tail alone and it would heal. He was right.) "Exotic," in veterinary terms, means anything that's not a cat, dog, or farm animal. Guinea pigs may not seem that fancy to you, but for some reason they count as exotics in the pet world. Same with hamsters, rats, birds, turtles, and animals that actually *do* seem exotic: iguanas, prairie dogs, hedgehogs, and snakes.

I've even read about vets who treat fish. Patients— no, wait, I guess the *fish* are the patients—*people* put their fish into water-filled containers and FedEx them to these vets, who perform all their exams and procedures underwater. No, wait, I guess only the *fish* are underwater. As you can see, I don't know a whole lot about what fish veterinarians do.

Maybe someday I'll commission a new mural that shows all the different vets who've helped our other animals:

Snips, our turtle. Snips got an infection in his shell. I might not have known anything was the matter except that his shell started to *stink.* When I picked him up, his shell seemed softer and sort of slimy, so I took him to a reptile vet.

It must be hard to be a vet when people tell you they'll pay only up to a certain amount for their pets to be treated. "Just do the minimum," people will say. "Don't go overboard trying to save Fluffster if it's going to cost too much." No one says this to a pediatrician. And vets love their patients just as much as pediatricians love theirs. I have a rule that all my pets deserve vet care, no matter how small they are. And I try never to ask how much a procedure for one of my pets will cost.

Still, I was surprised when I picked Snips up at the vet's a week later. "He had to be on an IV drip in his foot for a few days," the vet's receptionist told me. She didn't explain how you get a tube into the foot of an animal who can pull his feet back into his shell, but I bet it's not easy. "And," she continued, "we had to shave off part of his shell." The cost for the week: more than a thousand dollars.

When another of my turtles got sick, though, this same vet adopted him. "I don't know if he'll get better," he said, "and I don't want to charge you when his condition is so iffy. Let me just keep him with my other turtles." A few months later, he proudly showed me that our turtle was living in a pond the vet had built in his own yard. For all I know, he's still there.

Hedgie, our first hedgehog. I took Hedgie to the same vet who had treated Snips. This was before much was known about hedgehog care, and Hedgie finally died. The vet asked if he could perform an autopsy on Hedgie so that he could learn more about hedgehog anatomy. That would help him with other hedgehogs in the future. I said yes, of course. The autopsy revealed that Hedgie had had liver cancer—and also that he was a girl. We still think of him as a boy, though.

Blaze, Laura's rat. Rats are prone to cancer, and Blaze developed a tumor on his chest. Figuring he was going to die soon, I took him to a vet to be put to sleep. The vet said, "I've never operated on a rat, but I think I can take this tumor out. I'd like to try. I'll only charge you for the anesthesia I use—not for my time."

Poor Blaze was shaky and tired after his operation—and also much, much smaller. The tumor in his chest had been four inches long and as big around as a golf ball. As soon as he felt better, he went back to his old scampering, ratty ways. He lived for six more happy months. Rats live for only a few years, so that was a nice, long amount of extra time for Blaze.

Mojo, my rabbit. Like many dwarf-breed rabbits, Mojo has always had problems with his jaw. He's had a bunch of surgery, and every three months he has to have his teeth filed down or they'll grow in the wrong direction. The first time Mojo got an abscess in his jaw, I didn't recognize what was the matter until he was very, very sick. I took him to a rabbit vet, and I've always loved her for the way she told me about his condition.

"I'll do what I can," she said. "But when a rabbit's temperature is this low, it's usually a sign that he wants to leave us."

"He wants to leave us"—what a much, much better way of saying "I'm afraid he's going to die." She was preparing me for the worst, but very gently.

This vet did manage to cure Mojo. She cut the abscess out of his jaw and placed tiny antibiotic "beads" in the cavity to treat the infection. She gave him IV fluids and force-fed him for several days. But my best memory of her care was the way she warned me that she might not be able to cure him at all.

When I brought Mojo in for a follow-up appointment a few weeks later, the vet said, "We have a three-week-old baby rabbit who's looking for a home. His owners left him here because his leg was injured and they didn't want to pay for his treatment. I had to amputate his foot, and he's probably going to have to have the whole leg amputated when he's bigger. We've named him Stumper. Do you know anyone who might want to adopt him?"

She called one of her technicians, who brought out a tiny gray rabbit asleep in the palm of her hand. Did I know anyone who wanted to adopt him? I wonder if you can guess the answer.

"It was so funny when I took Mojo to the vet today," I told my husband an hour later. "Because he turned out to be pregnant, even though he's a boy, and here's the baby bunny that was inside his tummy!" That was how I introduced Stumper to the household.

For a few months, Stumper managed to hobble around on his little peg leg, but finally the stump started to hurt him when he walked. I tried putting a doll sock on it, but *you* try keeping a sock on a rabbit! Still, I hated the thought of putting Stumper through another amputation.

"He'll be okay," the vet reassured me. "You'll see—in a couple of days he won't even know his leg is missing."

She was right. Stumper's completely comfortable now. *He* doesn't know how funny he looks when he's running. *He* doesn't know that he has a little skirt of fur where the leg used to be. All he knows is that he can't scratch his ear on that side, and I have to help him.

And the vet didn't charge me for the surgery, which would have cost hundreds of dollars. "When you adopted

Stumper, I told you he would probably need another operation," she said. "I'm not going to ask you to pay for something that was the matter before you got him."

Vets deserve a lot of respect. Most of them work just as many hours as human doctors do, for less money. They take in all kinds of stray animals, too. Dr. Ferris and Dr. Mike adopted a huge cat who spends his days greeting the animals in their waiting room. "I'm so sorry you're not well," he seems to be saying as he walks from pet to pet. "And I'm so glad *I'm* well." They also have an adopted canary who sings (loudly) all day long.

The only bad memory I have of any vet is a man who shouted "NO! *NO!*" at one of my prairie dogs. She had a bump on her forehead, and she kept twisting out of the way when he tried to examine her. I would think a vet, of all people, would know that yelling at a prairie dog will not make her behave! But he did cure the bump, so I forgave him.

lost! (and usually found)

The first pet I ever owned myself was a hamster named Finally—because I *finally* got him, you see. Oh, no, wait—Finally wasn't my first pet. My first pet was a turtle my parents gave me when I was five. His name was Yurtle (not as good a name, but come on—I was only in kindergarten!), and after about two weeks I completely forgot to feed him. In fact, I completely forgot about Yurtle, period. When I was seven, I suddenly asked my mother, "Whatever happened to that turtle I had?" My mother said he had died, and she and my father had buried him in secret. Obviously I wasn't old enough to take care of a pet back then. Let's not talk about it anymore.

So anyway, my hamster Finally. When I was in third grade, I had a weird obsession with some bee-shaped brooches that were advertised in *The New Yorker* magazine every week. Looking at them in my mind now, I see that they must have been horribly ugly—but back then, how I longed for one! They had gold legs and wings, and the bodies were made from artificial star sapphires. I loved thinking about those artificial star sapphires so much. Every time I saw the ad in the magazine, I would open my parents' big encyclopedia and lustfully stare at the star sapphire on the "Precious Gems" page. Then I'd pore over the ad some more. Then I'd count the money I'd saved. Then, back to the encyclopedia picture. The brooches were eighteen dollars, which seemed like an impossible amount of money. And it *was* kind of impossible with my allowance set at thirty-five cents a week—but at last, somehow, I'd scraped the eighteen dollars together. And then my mother said I couldn't buy one of those brooches.

I don't know who was right. Actually, I do know—*I* was. It was my money, and I'd saved it, and I should have been able to buy whatever I wanted with it except for a bow and arrow, which I also wanted. On the other hand, I can see my mother's point. An eight year old wearing a large, fake-sapphire, bee-shaped brooch to school would just have been asking for trouble. And I know I would have worn that brooch to school, because of some of the other things I can remember wearing to school. For example, I once fastened a troll-head keychain to the button of my shirt and wore *it* to school. When some boys in my class (David Lee and Peter Elliott) made fun of it, I lied and said that I had been given the troll head when I was born. You know what? Let's not talk about *that* anymore, either.

But now I had eighteen dollars to spend on anything I wanted except a bee brooch. My mother had no problem with my getting a hamster, and I ended up loving Finally even more than I would have loved the star-sapphire bee. So maybe my mom was right after all! (Except she wasn't.)

At least I could do more with a hamster than I could with a brooch. I wrote a story about Finally—well, the last sentence, anyway. It was "Finally sat down and nonchalantly began to wash his face." I couldn't figure out how to lead up to that sentence, but I was sure the story would be great once I'd thought of a way. I also drew a lot of educational posters about hamsters, always carefully illustrating the way you could tell a boy hamster from a girl hamster. When my parents were having dinner at the house of some friends who were very into health food, I asked if they would please ask their friends for some wheat germ for Finally. They wouldn't, though.

FINALLY'S VOYAGE

Like many hamsters, Finally was an escape artist, although I don't think he ever escaped from his cage. His getaways were always during these marathon exercise sessions I used to give him, when I'd take him out of his cage and let him run around the basement for a couple of hours. Considering how much I loved him, you'd think I would have kept better track of him—but somehow I always lost him. Usually I'd find him after a few minutes. He'd be hiding under my dad's workbench or behind a pile of old *Life* magazines in the corner. But one afternoon, Finally was just *gone*.

Of course I felt terrible, and of course I looked for him all over the place. Everyone did. No one liked the idea that Finally might have gotten into one of the walls of the house. But when we'd searched every inch of the basement without luck, we decided that's what must have happened.

Three mornings later, when my mother pulled back the shower curtain in one of the second-floor bath-rooms, Finally was standing on the bottom of the tub looking up at her. We never figured out how he had got-ten in there, but he was fine. And I kept a better eye on him after that.

A couple of years later, though, after Finally had died, my father pulled back some old boards in the cellar and found a massive pile of seeds and shredded newspapers. It was like a secret hamster camp. Every time he'd been loose in the basement, Finally must have stashed a few supplies behind the boards in case he needed them. I like to imagine him thinking, "I don't even need those

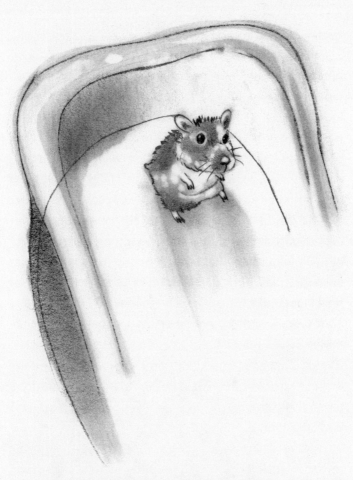

humans anymore. I'm *completely* independent. Or I will be, as soon as they let me out of this cage."

Over the years since then, I've lost a lot of animals, but most of them have come back home one way or another.

SNIPS'S KITCHEN ADVENTURE

When my kids were little, we got our turtle Snips. The children named him Snips, because "Snaps" seemed too violent, and anyway, he wasn't a snapping turtle; he was a red-eared slider. Snips started out in a tank on our kitchen table so we could watch him swim—until I realized that what we were mostly doing was watching him poop into the water. Even *my* family doesn't necessarily want to see that during breakfast. And glass aquariums full of water are so hard to lift. So we put Snips into the bathtub in our first-floor bathroom, with a heat lamp set up so he could bask in its rays when he wanted to.

He was always a bit of a surprise for our guests. They'd walk into the bathroom and there would be a

sliding splash as Snips hurled himself off his little plastic floating island into the water. Little kids sometimes wouldn't use that bathroom at all. One four-year-old visitor burst into tears when her mother said it was time for a bath. "The turtle will annoy me!" she wailed, not realizing that her bath was going to be in a different bathroom. The tub worked great for Snips, though—and for me, because it's much easier to empty a bathtub than a glass aquarium.

Why did my kids and I decide Snips needed exercise one afternoon, and bring him into the kitchen? I have no idea. Maybe we wanted to see what the dogs would do when they saw him. In any case, the instant we got a little bored and stopped standing guard over Snips, he raced under the refrigerator. And I mean *raced*. You hear about turtles being slow, but when they want to get away they move a lot faster than you'd think. The tiny wet tracks of Snips's nails on the kitchen floor were the only sign of him.

Normally, this would be the kind of time I'd call my husband to come down and give us a hand. Unfortunately, David was out of town, so I had to use my own brain. In a situation like this I always think, "Why do I have to be a grownup? Why can't my mom and dad take care of the problem?" But there were my own children looking up at me wide-eyed, and I had to pretend I was in control.

In the end it was easier than I'd expected. I got a broom, and I gave Laura a yardstick. Using them sort of like chopsticks, we poked them under the refrigerator and swept Snips—scrabbling frantically with his little claws—out into the open. When he got back into the bathtub, he stayed underwater for a long, long time.

We lost Snips again when we moved out of our house one summer. We were having a new kitchen and some new bathrooms put in, and we couldn't live in the house while the construction was going on. So we rented another house that had a barn in the back yard. Our birds' and prairie dogs' cages went into the barn, the dogs lived in the rented house with us, and the rabbits lived in the basement. I drove back to our real house twice a day to feed the cats. They were very upset about the construction crew, but not as upset as they would have been if we had made them move with us for the summer.

The rental house didn't have a spare bathtub, so we put Snips in a huge tank in the yard. He liked being out in the sunshine, I think, instead of having to bask under the heat lamp I had attached to his old bathtub. But one day there was a flash flood in our town while we were away for the weekend. It rained and rained and rained and rained and rained—and Snips's tank overflowed. He floated right out over the side and walked away in the rain.

The rental house was near a couple of ponds and a slow-moving river, so if Snips got to one of those spots he was probably okay. I felt terrible to have lost him. And yet I liked the thought of his walking away through the wet grass, savoring freedom for the first time in his life. I hope his instincts took him to water and that he's still alive, living on minnows and insects and wild food the way he was meant to do.

Speaking of Snips's bathroom, I once went in there in the middle of the night and found a flying squirrel scuffling around in one corner. It must have come down our chimney. (David caught it in a towel and put it outside.) As I'm typing this, a bat has been loose in our house for three days now. It, too, may have come down the chimney, or perhaps flown in when a door was open. The bat comes out and flaps around at night, but we haven't been able to catch it yet. We even left the doors open and tried to wave the bat outside, but it wouldn't go. And when we come down in the morning it's hidden itself somewhere behind a picture or in the bookcase where we can't find it. It's very disconcerting. I keep thinking I see the bat over my shoulder. Then I whip around and find that I'm looking at a shadow.

But those aren't examples of animals *escaping*. Let's see, who else?

VACATION ESCAPES

A lot of my animal horror stories are connected to times my family has gone on trips and I've decided I can't leave one or another pet behind. Once, I brought my first prairie dog, Buttercup, on a visit to my parents' house. We put her cage in the laundry room, which was in the basement. My parents were having a big party that night, and some kids at the party stupidly let Buttercup loose. My parents' basement is a labyrinth of rooms and workbenches and tables and old Twister games and jelly jars and extra paper towel rolls, and I was afraid I'd never see Buttercup again. I called and called, and finally I heard a sleepy squeak from one corner. Buttercup had crawled into a suitcase and gone to sleep.

Our rabbit Mojo got lost when I brought him along on a family vacation. We were staying in a little cabin at a family camp, and I set up a pen for Mojo in one corner. I arranged the pen around a bed, so that Mojo could hide under the bed when he felt like being in a burrow. The kids at the camp kept wanting to come in and visit him, but I said they could do it only when I was in the cabin.

One morning I came back from the beach to find that Mojo was missing. He wasn't under the bed; he was nowhere in the cabin; he was nowhere outside that I

could see. Frantic, I ran up to the first group of kids I saw and said, "Where's Mojo? What did you guys do with him?" Without waiting for an answer, I rushed back to the cabin—where I heard a thumping, rattling sound. Mojo had torn the bed's mattress open and crawled up inside the springs. He must have thought that the inside of the bed made an even better burrow than the floor underneath it. Of course, I had to apologize to the kids I'd yelled at.

A FROG MAKES HIS GETAWAY

Then there was our white frog, Alviney. (Laura named him when she was five. She was a little confused about the word *albino*.) Alviney started out normal size and quickly became much too thin because we were mistakenly giving him the wrong kind of food. Once I found the right kind—African frog food—he ballooned to the size and shape and general appearance of a tennis ball.

One day Alviney's glass aquarium cracked, and we transferred him to a bowl while I went to find another aquarium. In that short time, Alviney jumped out of the bowl, flopped his way across the porch floor, and squeezed out under the screen. I'd like to think he made

his way to freedom. But I have an awful feeling that a fat white frog hopping through the green grass was kind of, well, *obvious* to any hawks or crows flying overhead. Anyway, we never saw him again.

JIMMY'S JOURNEY

We had better luck with our cat Jimmy. Jimmy had been found as a six week old. A man in a supermarket parking lot kept hearing a cat meowing but couldn't see one. When he'd driven home, he still heard the meowing. He checked underneath his car—and there was a tiny black-and-white kitten. Jimmy was frantically holding on to the car's undercarriage with his gigantic paws. (Jimmy has seven claws on one front paw and six on the other.) The man brought him to an animal shelter, where he was quickly adopted and given his name. But a year later, the woman who'd adopted him married someone who was allergic to cats. Back Jimmy went to the shelter, and we read about him in our newspaper.

We adopted Jim because he was so friendly. When you held your hand out to him, he would grab it in his paws and drag it up to his mouth to give you some little love bites. I realize that doesn't sound so friendly, but it is. The shelter directors said Jimmy needed to spend lots of time outside. They thought he'd do fine with our cat setup, where each cat has its own little house next to our front and back doors. But we hadn't counted on Jimmy's being so freaked out that he'd run away within the first hour.

I was furious with our other two cats. Couldn't they have been a little nicer to Jimmy? I was angry with Beanie, too. Beanie was just a puppy then, and when we introduced him to Jimmy, Beanie let out the first barks he had ever barked. They weren't very loud— more like little squawks—but I was still mad at him. "You should have welcomed Jimmy!" I wanted to say.

Mostly, I was mad at myself for having put poor Jimmy into this situation.

Our town's animal warden tried to cheer us up. "He's probably not far away," she told us. "I bet he's hanging around on the edge of your property. He'll come closer when he gets really hungry." I put dishes of food out in the yard and hoped that she was right. But for three weeks, there was no sign of our new cat.

I had pretty much given up when I heard a cat meowing frantically in the woods one night. I recognized that high, shrill, rapid meow. About the only thing I knew about Jimmy—from picking him up at the animal shelter—was that his meow is more like a kitten's than a cat's.

"Jimmy?" I called—and he slowly crept out of the woods toward me.

I guess he had finally had enough of being alone in the woods. He let me pick him up and bring him into the laundry room. He purred frantically the whole time, and he wouldn't stop rubbing me with his head. Anyone could have seen how relieved he was to have given up his independence.

I couldn't bring him any farther into the house than the laundry room because of David's allergies. Instead, I brought a sleeping bag and pillow into the laundry room so I could be near Jimmy all night long. I put some food and water and a litter box next to us. Jimmy squeezed into the sleeping bag and stayed next to me all night. I don't know what the newspaper delivery man thought the next morning when he saw us lying there on the laundry room floor. But I didn't care. The next day, Jimmy stayed put in the yard. He moved in to his own cat house and ate his meals along with the other cats.

That was seven years ago, and Jimmy has never left our yard again.

pecky the owl

There's something about owls that speaks to us.

Here's a little educational paragraph, just in case you think I'm lying: The ancient Greeks used a coin that had an owl on one side and the goddess Athena on the other. In Japan, small owl figurines were once used to ward off disease and hunger. Samoans once believed that people were descended from an owl; and in parts of medieval France, women who wanted husbands would go to the woods and call out to owls for help. (I don't know if the owls were supposed to drop a husband at their feet, or what.) And surely you've heard the expression "as wise as an owl," though owls aren't in fact all that much smarter than other birds.

Why this fascination? It's got to be partly because owls are so mysterious; they come out only at night, and they fly silently. (The edges of their wing feathers have a special comblike fringe that muffles the sound of flapping.) But I think it's even more because owls look so human. Their eyes stare straight ahead, like people's eyes. Their shape, too, is more like a person's than a bird's. They stand straight on their short legs, like soldiers. They even turn their heads the way people do— slowly and deliberately, rather than the sideways darting motion most other birds use.

I thought I was lucky when we moved to our house in the country, where you can hear different owls all night long. I never thought I'd be lucky enough to meet a baby owl and get to take care of him. Then Pecky came into my life.

In back of our house are some huge white pines. From my office window, which is on the third floor of the house, I can watch all the birds that fill them. Blue jays take turns perching on the bare stump of one branch that must be fifty feet off the ground. I think they like being able to see so far. Downy woodpeckers scuttle up and down the tree trunks looking for insects. Once, a pileated woodpecker—the kind that looks like Woody—was out there tapping so loudly that it sounded like a hammer. Chickadees zoom in and out, doing whatever chickadees do. Then a couple of squirrels will rush from tree to tree, their tails whirling behind them as they chase each other, and all the birds will take off.

It never occurred to me that owls, too, might live in those pine trees, so close to our house—until we found a dead baby screech owl lying on the ground one day in summer. The poor thing was facedown, its wings spread out as though it had tried to stop its fall. It had most of its feathers but clearly not enough to fly with. We were all sad to see it, but happy, in a way, to know that an owl nest was nearby.

Something must have been going on with that nest. Maybe the mother owl had been delayed, and the babies, too hungry to sit still, tried to leave before they were ready. In any case, the next evening I found another baby owl in almost the same exact spot. He was lying facedown—but he was alive.

He was about as long as my hand and had grayish brown feathers. His chest was moving very faintly. His eyes were closed. I couldn't believe he would live, and I didn't want to hurt him. At the same time, I knew I might never again have the chance to see a baby owl this close. And certainly I couldn't leave him outside for the cats to find, if he was hurt.

One of the best things to do if you find a baby bird is to make it a new nest out of a light plastic flowerpot or a little basket. Line the pot with paper towel, gently put the baby in, and then hang the pot as near to the original nest as possible. The bird's parents will most likely find it and feed it. They won't "get your scent" and refuse to feed the baby, as people sometimes say. Birds don't have much of a sense of smell.

But these huge white pines didn't have any low branches I could have hung a pot from. In any case, I couldn't see a nest anywhere. So I put the owl into a cardboard box and brought him into the kitchen. Then the kids and I bent over to look at him more closely.

If a bird can't clench its toes, that often means its leg or its back is broken. To test the owl's reflexes, I stuck my finger under his foot. To my surprise, his claws— very thick, strong talons for such a small guy—curled tightly around my finger. I tried the other foot; same thing. Encouraged, I stretched out each of his wings, which still had their fluffy baby feathers. Pecky tucked them back neatly against his sides as soon as I let go. So his wings were okay, too.

I scratched the top of his head a little, and he opened his eyes and stared up at me. His eyes were round and yellow and blind-looking. He blinked a few times. Then he clumsily struggled to his feet.

What was I supposed to do now?

I stuck my hand under his feet experimentally and said, "Up, up," the way I always did with Japan. As if he understood me, the little owl clutched my hand with his toes and swung himself into a standing position.

He wasn't hurt at all! Before I could react, he had scrambled up my arm to perch on my shoulder. It was just what any tame parakeet would have done.

I don't think David has ever been as surprised as when I walked into his office with a baby owl on my shoulder and said, "Look what I've got."

As you know, it's a rule of my household that any animal crisis will happen at the least convenient time: when we're about to leave for vacation, at three in the morning, or on a weekend when all the vets' offices are closed and the nearest emergency animal clinic is two hours away. By the time Pecky was standing on my shoulder, it was ten-thirty at night—too late for me to call Banjie, who had to go to bed very early because all her baby birds would be getting up at dawn.

Fortunately, I own a bunch of spare cages, and I always have plenty of cat food in the house—not a perfect owl food, but better than nothing. I mushed some up and fed the owl a bite with my fingers. (Ugh.) He swallowed quickly, stared at me, and clacked his beak hungrily for more. I poked a few more fingerfuls into his beak, and then Pecky turned his head away. He kind of squinched down on his perch and closed his eyes.

I was too excited to go to bed myself. I washed a few dishes and then returned to Pecky's cage out in the porch. As I walked in, he straightened up and clacked his beak like a little set of castanets.

PECKY BECOMES THE BEST MEMBER OF OUR FAMILY, INCLUDING MY KIDS

Over the next few days, I became very familiar with that clacking sound. All the baby birds I've raised seem good at recognizing human voices. The baby robins, starlings, or blue jays on my kitchen counter always start screeching, "Feed me! Feed me!" when they hear me talking. Not in words, of course, but anyone can tell that's what they mean. Pecky didn't call; he clacked. He got to love cat food and mealworms, and when he was a few days older, he was able to eat a chicken drumstick using one foot while balancing on the other. (I know that sounds kind of cannibalistic—a bird eating another bird!—but you have to remember that owls are predators, and in the wild their prey includes birds.)

"This is your best animal ever," a friend said to me.

It did seem that way. My arms got all scratched up

from Pecky's talons, but I didn't care. (I wore leather gardening gloves on my hands, though. I *need* my hands.) If I lifted him and put him against my chest, Pecky would bury his face against me so I could scratch the top of his head. If I stopped scratching, he would slowly lift his head and stare up at me as if to say, "I might be sad, you know." (I'm sure he didn't *feel* sad, but his huge owl eyes made him look heartbroken.)

It's so, so tempting to keep a wild animal! Wildlife rehabilitators aren't supposed to spend too much time with their animal charges. They're not supposed to pat them or get to know them too well, because the animals might become too tame to be able to take care of themselves when they're released back into the wild. In my opinion, by the way, this is bogus. Wild animals become wild when they're old enough. They get plenty of physical contact from their mothers in the wild, and they don't get too tame to leave *them*. I think that baby mammals and baby birds need a generous amount of handling until they're almost grown.

But I do agree that you shouldn't try to keep a wild animal as a pet. It almost never works out well. At the same time, isn't it every animal lover's dream to keep a bunch of wild pets? Remember Dickon in *The Secret Garden*, with his tame crow and his tame fox cub and the squirrel that lived in his pocket? When I was a kid, that always seemed like magic to me. And once I'd had Pecky for a week, I was in love with him.

BUT, BUT, BUT . . .

"He'd really be better off staying with me," I would argue to myself. "We could build him a huge cage outside. He'd be safe and well-fed, and we'd get to see him all the time."

"Raccoons could get him if he's in a cage," my conscience would argue back.

"I'll make the cage *really* strong," I would tell my conscience.

"Why would Pecky like that more than being free?" my conscience would say.

And to that I wouldn't have an answer.

I knew, too, that he needed more than just plain meat and cat food to eat. Owls need to swallow their prey whole. Did you know that you can buy frozen baby mice for raptors (birds of prey) and snakes? I hated the idea of doing this, but I figured it was better than starting out with live animals. And I knew Pecky had to start eating on his own—not just clacking his beak for me to feed him.

So I got a product that was horribly named Mice on Ice. The package showed happy cartoon mice skating around; you peeled away the wrapper to pop out one mouse at a time. I kept my eyes almost closed while I did this, and pulled the frozen mouse out with a paper towel wrapped around my hand. Then I dropped it in the bottom of Pecky's cage and ran out of the room with— for some reason—my hands clapped over my ears.

I wish I could say, "And I came back in to find the frozen mouse all gone." In fact, I came back in to find that it was still there. Obviously Pecky couldn't "read" it as food because it wasn't alive. Was I going to have to get live mice for him to eat? I couldn't bear the thought.

My own conscience was bad enough. Then Pecky himself started sending me messages. He had begun to be able to fly short distances, but he always returned to his perch. One morning, though, I walked into the porch to see him standing on the floor looking out at the yard. He looked like a tiny man—a *sad* tiny man. He liked us fine, but anyone could see that he didn't want to be inside. Yet he was still too young to be turned loose on his own; there was no one to teach him how to hunt. What had I done?

A *REAL* MOM FOR PECKY

Every now and then, something perfect happens.

That afternoon I was out on the patio doing some weeding while Pecky watched from the porch. As I bent over to yank out a dandelion, a bird flew down and dive-bombed my head. I straightened up in time to see *another* screech owl flying away. She was a little larger than Pecky, and her feathers were smooth and adult looking, whereas his were still ruffly.

Nothing like that had ever happened to me before. It was still light out! I had never, ever seen an owl flying in the daytime. Not only that, but what were the odds of my coming into contact with two screech owls in the same month?

When the owl dive-bombed me again a second later, I realized that this couldn't be a coincidence. The second owl had to be Pecky's mother. She had figured out where Pecky was—she must have known all along—and she wanted him back.

I called Banjie. "The mother owl will start taking care of him again," she promised. "If she's trying to get him back, she still wants to raise him."

"So I should . . . I should just put him outside?"

"Wait until evening," Banjie advised. "He won't see as well during the daytime."

As soon as the sun began to set, I took Pecky on my hand and gave him one more scratch on the head. Then I carried him outside and set him on the highest branch I could reach.

Just before it was too dark to see, I went outside to check the branch. Two screech owls were sitting there—Pecky and the adult with smooth plumage. I knew she was his mother. She had found him again, and from now on she would take over.

The next morning, both owls had flown away.

Sometimes when I'm coming in late at night, I hear the quivering cry of a screech owl. I always wonder if it's Pecky. Just in case it is, I always tell him hello.

"Say hi to your mother," I add. "And tell her thanks for sharing you with me."

three hedgehogs

When I was in fourth grade, my teacher, Miss Swang, assigned us an essay about what we liked doing best. I wrote something called "The Care of Small Animals and Birds." In it I bragged, "I can make animal noises. Once, when I saw a squirrel in a tree, I 'squirrel talked' to him, and he came down the tree and got in my lap!"

That was a total lie, of course. I can't believe Miss Swang let me get away with it. But I still like to think that I can communicate with animals on a special level, a wordless level that other people can't manage. I always imagine that if I were to see—for example—a female grizzly bear in the forest, I would fix her with a calm, gentle stare that would say more than words possibly could. Not that words probably mean all that much to a bear. Anyway, she would understand that I meant no harm and would let me play with her cubs.

I got to test my animal-communication theory with the first hedgehog I ever saw. This was way back in 1991, before hedgehogs were common pets. I was interviewing the owner of an exotic-pet store called Parrots of the World and asked if I could hold one of the hedgehogs he had for sale. He said sure. It hurt to pick up the hedgehog—hedgehog spines feel exactly like twitching thumbtacks—but a lot of people were watching me, so I had to pretend I didn't care. I cradled the hedgehog in my hands and murmured soothingly to him. In a second, he unrolled and peeked out at me. He stopped twitching and began to relax. Even his spines seemed softer. Then he leaned over and bit me very hard on the thumb.

I guess that was a kind of communication, although I didn't like what he was saying.

I forgave the hedgehog, whom I bought soon afterward. Hedgie looked too much like a fairy-tale creature for me to stay mad at him. Asleep, hedgehogs are like spiny sea urchins. Awake, they're like windup toys with little dog noses, ears that look as if they're made out of gray felt, and tiny useless tails. They don't walk; they toddle. When they're scared, they make a noise that's exactly like a coffee percolator—but they mostly get scared only when you wake them up.

Hedgie didn't mind being woken up if you threw a few crickets into his tank. Then he'd explode with excitement. He would dart back and forth, banging into the sides of his tank and smudging the glass with noseprints. "I just *know* a cricket's in here somewhere!" he seemed to be saying. The crickets would bounce around him like popcorn. Once in a while, Hedgie managed to catch a cricket, but he was just as likely to grab a mouthful of bedding instead. He always gave up and went to sleep long before the crickets were gone. I think a few of the leftover crickets still live in our house.

Hedgie loved earthworms too, but I don't want to talk about that. It takes a hedgehog a long, noisy time to eat a worm.

A hedgehog's soft, fat little feet could get hurt on a regular exercise wheel, so I bought Hedgie a wheel made out of a special screen. All night he would slowly trudge along on it, and then in the morning he'd disappear under his bedding. That was about it for Hedgie's activities.

He did once pay a visit to a local school when a nine-year-old boy named Toby was presenting a project on hedgehogs to his class. It's hard for a shy animal to visit a bunch of kids. The kids are always so eager for the animal to *do* something that they can't help getting loud and excited. The main thing Hedgie seemed to want to "do" was demonstrate how good he was at staying rolled up in a ball. With a sudden rush of bravery, Toby patted Hedgie's nose with a finger. In response, Hedgie bit down on Toby's finger and held on like a little bulldog.

All the kids gasped and stepped quickly back. Toby flapped his hand frantically; Hedgie held on grimly. I don't know which of them I felt sorrier for.

I'm not all that reliable in a crisis. Once, my sister Nelie accidentally threw her Christmas stocking into the fire. My reaction: run out of the room screaming, just like the time I've already told you about when I was little and our dog picked up our parakeet in her mouth. And just as she had rescued the parakeet, my sister Cathy—my *younger* sister Cathy—rescued the stocking.

But I did manage to stay calm in the Hedgie crisis. "Slowly, *slowly* lower your hand to the desk," I brayed at

Toby above the noise of the other kids. I grinned mania-cally at him, as if we were all having a great time. "Hedgie is scared. He'll let go when he feels the desk under him."

And thank heaven he *did* let go, because I had only been guessing that was what he would do. I scooped him up, while he still percolated, and dropped him back into his tank. Whenever I showed Hedgie to kids after that, I always kept the lid on. (Toby was fine, by the way.)

But it's kind of fun having a pet who doesn't care about anything except eating and using an exercise wheel. Hedgehogs are like a cross between a museum exhibit that poops a lot and a teddy bear that has to be fed. You can just look at a hedgehog and not worry that he wants more attention. He won't miss you when you're on vacation; he won't care if you're too busy to talk to him. He doesn't miss other hedgehogs, either; hedgehogs are solitary creatures. A hedgehog is a per-fect "looking at" pet. When Hedgie died, I got a replace-ment named Prickelina.

PRICKELINA

By then I'd stopped buying animals in pet stores, so I bought Prickelina from a hedgehog breeder. Prickelina was much fancier than Hedgie. He had been brown, with gray ears; she was white, with pink ears. She was also much friendlier than Hedgie—at least for the first couple of days that we had her. If we called her name, she'd toddle out of her bed to investigate us. If we picked her up, she wouldn't roll into a hissing, spiny ball the way Hedgie had. (Hedgehogs roll up when they're frightened. A predator like a fox won't want to bite those spines.) She would cuddle against us and then try to climb up our arms.

Then we moved her into a big cage, and I swear she never spoke to us again. Immediately she turned just as grumpy as Hedgie had been. However, she continued to be a lovely adornment for our playroom.

PATTY RUTH

Hedgehogs don't live very long. Prickelina died when she was three, and then Patty Ruth came to live with us. It was almost as if Patty Ruth understood that she'd been named after two of my best friends, because she started out friendly and stayed that way right up until the end.

"I can't get her to roll up in a ball no matter how hard I try," her breeder wrote me. "She's too sweet."

I'm sure the breeder didn't try very hard. I mean, he didn't poke Patty Ruth or jostle her around or anything. But most hedgehogs roll up the instant you touch them. Patty Ruth never did that. She stayed relaxed and

"open" as long as you felt like holding her. She was just like Prickelina in the early days, except that she never turned grumpy. The other two hedgehogs had always clambered off their exercise wheels and hidden if you spied on them at night; Patty Ruth just kept marching along. If we put her on the floor, she would explore— poking her nose under toys, sniffing the edges of bookcases—instead of dashing under the sofa. Sometimes I even thought she was watching the birds in the cage next to hers, though it was hard to tell because a hedgehog's eyes don't have much expression.

And then, amazingly, Patty Ruth learned to talk! One morning I walked into the room to find her reading to the pygmy mice!

No, I didn't. Sorry. Patty Ruth never got *that* interesting. But she was a dear little darling, and I miss her a lot. Whenever I pass her grave—which is under a tree in our back yard, next to two of the prairie dogs—I say I love her. I say it right out loud.

aliens in the house

Not everyone would like keeping caterpillars the size of a man's thumb in cages on their porch. But my cecropia caterpillars always start out the size of grains of rice. That fools me into thinking, "Oh, they'll be easy to take care of." They never are, but when they turn into moths, it's always worth it.

Cecropias are members of the giant silkworm moth family—the largest moths in the United States. If there's a bigger moth somewhere, I don't want to meet it. With their wings outspread, cecropias measure six inches across. Their markings are just as amazing as their size. Their frosty brown wings are adorned with crescent shapes and eyespots and bordered with a red stripe. They have furry red-and-white-striped bodies and furry red legs. They live mostly in the woods, and like all moths, they come out only at night. So you're not likely to see one close up unless you raise them yourself.

As I said, cecropia larvae start out the size of grains

of rice—fuzzy black rice. The eggs are even smaller, about the size of those round cupcake sprinkles that are sometimes called "hundreds and thousands." I always put the eggs in a milk-carton cap on top of a few fresh lilac leaves, so that the instant the eggs hatch the larvae will be able to start eating. At that point, the babies are so delicate that the only way to transfer them to a fresh leaf is to use a very fine watercolor brush. It's a worrisome process. What if I slip and my hand smashes down on them? Or what if I drop them and they blow away? So far I've been pretty lucky. But whenever I have to move them, I sweat a lot until it's over.

The tiny larvae don't stay black and fuzzy for long. They shed their skins every couple of weeks for two months. After the first shedding (which entomologists call an "instar"), they're bright yellow with black bristles. That's when I start thinking of them as caterpillars instead of larvae.

Watching caterpillars shed their skins is like watching a movie about aliens. For a day or so, the caterpillars stop eating or even moving much: they're busy attaching their back legs to a leaf with a little silk pad. When they're securely fastened to the leaf, they begin wriggling. They writhe and twist until the

skin suddenly splits across their "shoulders." Then they peel themselves out of it the way you'd step out of a wet bathing suit. Once, John and I saw a caterpillar *lift off its old head* with its two front legs.

The caterpillars leave the old husk of a skin on the leaf and march away in their bright new clothes. With the second shedding, they turn green. After that, they get greener and brighter and more alien looking each time. When they're finally finished shedding, they're HUGE— four or five inches long, and as thick as a cigar. They look exactly as if they're made of green plastic. Along their sides are rows of bright-blue dots. Down their backs run two lines of bright-yellow dots with black bristles, like miniature cactus spines. And on their heads are four red dots with black spines, like thorned ladybugs.

When the cecropias are still tiny larvae, you can hardly believe they're eating at all. You'll see one at the tip of a lilac leaf; six hours later it's *still* at the tip of the lilac leaf, which still seems to be exactly the same size. When the caterpillars are at their largest, you can hear them chewing if you listen carefully. You can also hear

their poop falling onto the floor of the cage. (You might like to know that caterpillar poop is called frass. We named our first cecropia caterpillar Frassy.) One leaf will last several larvae a couple of days. By the time they've changed their skin a few times, each caterpillar will go through several leaves daily. They're absolutely *relentless* eaters.

"So what's the problem?" you may be asking. "All you have to do is give them new leaves every day."

Here's the problem: the leaves they need aren't always where *you* happen to be. I used to raise luna moth caterpillars. Lunas are my favorite moth because they're so beautiful—a misty pale green that's almost transparent. The word "luna" means moon, and they do look like the kind of moth you'd see in a moonscape. All my life—ever since reading a book called *Then There Were Five*, by Elizabeth Enright, when I was in fifth grade—I had longed to see one. In that book, Oliver Melendy, who's eight, spots a luna moth on his bedroom window screen one night. "A luna!" Oliver exclaims. "I never thought I'd see a real luna!"

But *Then There Were Five* was written in 1944. If lunas were rare back then, how likely was I to spot one? I had never expected to, until (like Oliver in the book) I moved to the country. Then, one Memorial Day weekend, I found two lunas on my garage door. Now I knew they were out there, and I couldn't relax until I got my hands on some luna eggs.

It's a problem that lunas like hickory leaves more than any other kind. There are tons of trees around my house but not a lot of hickories. I had to go deep into the woods to find them, which meant the leaves always started way high up on the trees. Sometimes I'd have to climb a tree to reach usable leaves. I'm a terrible tree climber, and I was always afraid that if anyone saw me they'd think I was stealing leaves for some reason. What was I going to do? *Explain?*

So I gave up on lunas and started raising cecropias. Cecropias' lilac and apple leaves are easier to find, but I have to take my caterpillars on vacation with me if I want to keep watching them grow. Also, to be honest, I can't quite believe someone else can take as good care of them as I do. I'm always afraid a pet sitter will squish them by mistake. This means I have to keep looking for leaves along the way. "Stop the car!" I'll suddenly yell. "I see an apple tree!" My kids used to get embarrassed when I'd pick lilac leaves outside rest stops. It made me look even crazier than I am.

When the caterpillars are finally big enough, they . . . what do they do, class? That's right! They make cocoons! Or, as insect people would say, "They cocoon." With some butterfly caterpillars, this is a big deal. The monarch caterpillar, for instance, coats itself with a beautiful, smooth jade green chrysalis speckled with gold dots. Not cecropias! They just roll themselves up inside an old leaf and forget about it. In the wild, their cocoons are usually camouflaged among the dead leaves at the base of the tree where they lived. In my porch, they just lie on the bottom of the tank. I position a couple of sticks in the tank so that the emerging moths will have something to hang from. Then I basically forget about them all winter. Once or twice a month I may mist them with a little water, but there's nothing else to do except wait.

In late spring, when the lilac and apple leaves outside are big enough for a caterpillar to eat, I start checking my cocoons daily. (Or hourly, or sometimes every few minutes if I'm bored.) Usually it takes a couple of really warm early-summer days before the moths emerge.

They crawl quickly out of their shriveled, ugly leaf casing. On trembling matted legs they walk up the sticks I've positioned in the cage. Their crumpled, wet wings hang down like old flags, and their bodies are so thick they're almost round. Slowly, and then faster, they start opening and closing their wings. The task facing them is to dry and harden their wings by pumping the fluid from their bodies into the wings; otherwise they won't be able to fly at all. When you think about it, it must be very hard work. As I've noticed with so many animals, being born is a huge, huge job. And in the wild, these caterpillars need to work fast before a bird can notice them and gobble them up.

But after their wings have dried and hardened, the moths have only one more thing to do. They won't eat again as long as they live—which will be just a couple of days. What they want now is to find a mate so that they can start the whole process over again.

The main way you can tell a male cecropia from a female is by the antennae. A male's antennae are wide and feathery; a female's are wispier. If I have a group of males and females, they'll mate in the tank. If I only have females, no problem! I put the tank outside on my patio and leave it there for the night.

Then yet another alien occurrence takes place. The female moths send out chemicals called pheromones that basically say "Hey, I'm ready to lay eggs!" to any male cecropias in the area. In quite a big area, actually: males can detect the pheromones from up to five miles away. The males start showing up at around eleven at night. The next morning, several wild male cecropias will have gathered on top of the tank to mate with the females. They look like bows on top of a present. Think of it—moths you would never know existed have flown into the open, into danger, just to meet girls!

The females lay eggs all over the tank. I collect the eggs, put them into a milk-carton cap with some fresh leaves, and wait for the process to start again. "It's okay," I tell myself when the new cecropias hatch. "They're so tiny that this won't take any work at all."

THE STUPIDEST THING I'VE EVER SAID ABOUT AN ANIMAL

I've had so many pets for so long that I've come to think I'm quite the animal expert. Sometimes this has bad consequences.

Once I took Laura and John to the Museum of Science in Boston. One of the museum's attractions is a big beehive. You can watch the worker bees, the drones, the cells filled with bee larvae, the cells filled with honey—everything that's in a normal hive, and it's all safely tucked behind glass so the bees can't get at you.

As we watched, a boy about six years old shoved up next to us. "Which one is the queen?" he asked.

"Oh, honey," I said in my most educational voice. "The queen is big and white, with no wings. We won't be seeing the queen today."

The boy shot me a scornful look. "*There* she is!" he said, pointing. And when I checked the guide next to the hive, I saw that he was right.

The queen bee looked a lot like the other bees, only much bigger. And he had picked her out instantly.

"Let's go see the butterfly exhibit now," I said to my kids.

voley

"Oh, no," I said to Laura one Friday afternoon. "One of the cats killed a baby vole."

I've always told my kids that squeamishness is the most useless emotion. It gets in the way of whatever you have to do. (Or, more often, it gets in the way of whatever you have to clean up.) But I'm not great at taking my own advice when it comes to staring down at dead animals. Seven-year-old Laura, on the other hand, bent right down in the grass to look at the casualty. "He's not dead, Mom!" she said.

And that's how Voley—or "the Little Gentleman," as my husband always called him—came to live with us.

Have you ever seen a vole? Probably not, unless you live in a rural area. I had never been close to a live one before, though our cats had caught several of them and left their bodies on the lawn. (Thanks a lot, cats.) Voles are little rodents about four inches long. They're a soft grayish brown, with inch-long tails and teeny flat ears.

They're rounder and fluffier and kinder looking than mice. Maybe that's why picture books about the Town Mouse and the Country Mouse often show a vole as the Country Mouse.

In 1872, Christina Rossetti published a poem that makes me think of Voley whenever I read it.

The city mouse lives in a house;—
The garden mouse lives in a bower,
He's friendly with the frogs and toads,
And sees the pretty plants in flower.

The city mouse eats bread and cheese;—
The garden mouse eats what he can;
We will not grudge him seeds and stalks,
Poor little, timid, furry man.

Our poor little, timid, furry man was unconscious when we first found him. He was tiny—maybe two inches long—and had probably left his mother's nest only a short time before. No wonder he passed out when a cat picked him up and dropped him! But there were no bite marks on his body. Within an hour he was scurrying around the spare cage we put him in, picking up birdseed and twinklingly looking out at us.

To tell you the truth, I couldn't stand to put him back outside. He was so small, and I was afraid the cats would just find him again. "Let's keep him for the weekend, until he's stronger," I said. Somehow the weekend kept being extended, and finally I got Voley a big tank and an exercise wheel and added him to our lineup of pets in the playroom.

"*Microtus pennsylvanicus!*" exclaimed a doctor who once visited our house and recognized Voley. (*Microtus pennsylvanicus*, the vole's scientific name, means "small-eared animal of the field.") "He's beautiful," the doctor added admiringly. I wouldn't say Voley was beautiful, but he was awfully nice. He didn't even mind being picked up and patted, and he never bit any of us. Male voles are less cranky than females, but even so, the way Voley kept his teeth to himself was unusual.

As I said earlier, wild animals rarely make good pets. Usually, they're just prisoners. But Voley was an exception. He became as tame as our hamsters within a couple of weeks, and he never tried to escape. If we came up to his tank, he'd rustle up from his nest and stare at us through the glass instead of burrowing to get away. Living in a cage may even have been healthier for him than being outside. In the wild, voles usually don't live for longer than a few months. Voley lived to be almost three years old.

For almost all that time, he looked the same. Then, suddenly, he was ancient. All the rodents I've owned seem to shrink as they get older. No matter how much they eat, they can't stop losing weight. We started giving Voley high-calorie treats like nuts and cereal, but he kept getting skinnier and skinnier. His toenails also grew very long—maybe because he wasn't running on his exercise wheel as much. He would slowly walk around his cage on tiptoe, looking feeble and shriveled. Still, it was a shock when we found him dead in his nest one morning.

The borders of our back yard are dotted with animal graves. Now it was time to add Voley. His coffin was a cookie box—John's choice. We lined the box with paper towel, but my husband, who had come down from his office to join us at the funeral, wasn't satisfied with that. Voley had always been one of David's favorites. He covered the paper towel with soft grass before we put Voley in.

When the kids were little, they liked to put some of the pets' favorite foods in the grave before we filled it up. (Our rat Blaze got a big handful of cheese puffs when he was buried.) John and Laura sprinkled some seeds around Voley's box, and then we covered it with dirt.

"Goodbye, Little Gentleman," David said.

quaker—the mistake?

I first met Quaker when a friend and I went to a pet store so she could buy some toys for her parrot Eli. This was one of the okay pet stores, where the owner really cares about the animals and does her best to keep them happy while they're with her. Still, there are going to be some unhappy animals in even the best pet stores. Quaker seemed pretty dejected when I spotted her.

She looked like a robin-sized bald eagle, with a sharp, bright orange beak, black body feathers, and upstanding white feathers on her head. The cage was only big enough for her to flap her wings in or jump from her perch to the floor, and she was sort of hunched up.

"What kind of bird is this?" I asked. I had never seen anything like Quaker before.

"A white-capped bulbul," the store owner told me. "They're from China."

"What do they eat?"

"Fruit, pellets, and some live food. We feed her wax-worms."

Ugh. Waxworms.

Waxworms are the white, grublike moth larvae of the wax moth. They're about an inch long and very, very, very, very soft. If you pick one up too hard, it will leave a bruise on the worm's velvety skin. On the other hand, they're easy to find at most pet stores—you can also order 1,000 at a time online, if you want—and you can keep them in the refrigerator. When they're cold, they go dormant and just lie there instead of squirming fatly around.

It's nice if you have a separate refrigerator for things like this. When I was little, my friend Muffy's brother put a bag of mealworms for his lizard into their family's refrigerator. The bag ripped, and the mealworms fell out and burrowed into a cake on the shelf underneath. Anyway, I *do* have a refrigerator for my pet foods. All I'd have to do with the waxworms would be to shake a few chilled worms into a dish, put them into Quaker's cage, and run away with my hands covering my eyes.

"Could she live in a flight cage with my other birds?" I asked the clerk. "I have canaries, parakeets, and finches. I don't have space for another flight cage."

I didn't like the look of Quaker's beak, which so clearly seemed to say "jabbing tool." I was half hoping the clerk would tell me, "No, it's out of the question. She needs to be alone." Then I'd be able to say, "I guess I can't buy her."

"I don't think that would be a problem" was the clerk's answer instead. "Just make sure to mist her with a plant mister every day. She loves having a bath."

I looked at Quaker, hunched on her perch. I knew that you should always carefully research a pet's needs before you buy it. (Can you afford its food? Will it need lots of vet checkups?) You should resist exotic species, especially: buying them will only encourage the store to collect more of them. More people will buy them and the misery will spread. And so on and so on.

"I'll take her," I said before I could change my mind.

FREAKED OUT

I worried all the way home, while Quaker sat quietly on the floor of the car in a little cardboard box the pet store had provided. Buying a pet on impulse was something I thought I had outgrown. In fact, I had pretty much decided not to get any more pets *ever*. "I should be giving more attention to the animals I have already," I scolded myself. "Now I'll have to spread my attention even thinner!"

But you can't return a pet. At least I can't. What, go back to the store and say, "Sorry, I changed my mind"? Sometimes people return pets by claiming that someone in their family "turned out to be" allergic to the new animal. I scorn this. Besides, the store where I'd bought Quaker was, like, an hour away from my house. There was no way around it—I was stuck with her.

I had that bad feeling *you* might have had when you walked into class on the first day of school and looked around thinking, "*These* are the kids in my class?" Your parents tell you that you'll make plenty of friends, but it's impossible to believe. In the same way, I was almost sure that Quaker and I would never get used to each other.

My doubts continued when I shook Quaker out of the box into the big flight cage. You could tell right away that she was going to be a tough fit for the other birds. For one thing, there was her method of flying. My canaries, parakeets, and finches liked to flutter gently from perch to perch. They would ruffle their feathers a bit, shake their wings a bit, maybe splash a bit in their bath—but nothing extreme.

Quaker flies like a dive-bomber, swooshing and zigzagging and making huge, dramatic landings. This is probably because in the wild, bulbuls chase a lot of insects. I could see how happy she was to have space to do some real flying, but her new roommates were not pleased by the intrusion. They froze into immobility on their perches, watching her with tilted heads. They were probably afraid to draw any attention to themselves, because Quaker looked just like a bird of prey. Which, in her own small way, she was.

Then there was the noise she made. For the first few days, Quaker was completely silent. Once she relaxed, she started to develop a variety of songs. Not songs, exactly—more like loud, harsh noises. Her most dreadful call was a squealing cry, sort of like a kitten stuck in a tree. For the first few days, she made this sound a lot. I would rush to her cage, worried that something was the matter. But Quaker would just be standing there, looking around. She wasn't upset about anything; that was just her normal sound. The other birds would be silently regarding her. None of their usual chirps and chattering with this alien in the cage!

Other noises Quaker liked (and still likes) to make:

- A rhythmic one-two, one-two, one-two-three meowing quack. "Quick-quick! Quick-quick! Quick-quick-quick!" Over and over and over.

- A rhythmic one-two-three, one-two-three, just for variation, with each note very slightly higher than the previous one. We pretend Quaker is counting for a waltz when she does this.

- A chirp that sounds like the word "Reyk-javík." "Rake-ya-vík! Rake-ya-vík!" When-ever Quaker makes this noise, I like to call out "Quaker, what's the capital of Iceland?" "Reykjavík," she answers. Loudly. *All* of Quaker's noises are made at top volume. You can hear her two floors away.

- She's also got a pretty, flute-y call that sounds like "doot-dootle-doot." It's so melodic that I sometimes suspect Quaker is actually a boy. Female birds don't usually sing as well as males. But I'm going to keep thinking of her as a girl, because that's what we're all used to.

Since my other birds are comparatively quiet, Quaker's loud singing was quite a distraction at first. Japan, my cockatiel, had sometimes whooped loudly, but at least you could tell what he meant by it. He was asking where I was, or—if he heard the dogs barking—he was saying, "Hey, something's going on some-where!" Quaker's sounds were impossible to decipher. I assumed that if she was making noise at all, she was probably at least feeling healthy. But even that was just a guess.

I looked bulbuls up on the Internet, hoping to learn enough to make Quaker more comfortable. There were lots and lots of pages about bulbuls in the wild. Red-whiskered bulbuls, red-crested bulbuls, dark-capped bul-buls. Violet-eared bulbuls, even. Where were *Quaker's* type of bulbul? It took a long time before I found any information about her species. And the only Web site I did find said that the bulbul's pet quality is "zero." This meant, basically, "There is nothing you can do to tame a bulbul or make it happy being around you."

So there we were, trapped together. Quaker didn't enjoy being a pet, and we didn't enjoy having her as a pet. But somehow we would have to make it work. After all, birds live a long time.

AND NOW?

It's been three years since Quaker moved in with us. I make sure to mist her with fresh water every day, and I give her as many brightly colored fruits as I can find. (Blueberries, cherries, and kiwi are her favorites.) Quaker really cares about color. Her fruit-flavored pellets come in green, yellow, red, and orange; they look like chopped Froot Loops. Bird experts say it's not a good idea for a bird to eat all that food coloring, but I've never been able to switch Quaker to plain brown pellets, even though they taste exactly the same. Moreover, she's so picky that she only likes the red and orange pellets—not the green and yellow ones. I've tasted all four colors. They certainly all taste the same to *me*, and I think Quaker just likes the red and orange ones because they look more fruitlike to her. I usually give her new pellets every day, so that she has a nice stock of her favorite colors. Once, as an experiment, I didn't put in new pellets for a few days. I wanted to see if Quaker would finally try the green and yellow pellets. At the end of five days, she had picked out *every single* red and orange pellet, leaving a dish of solid green and yellow. She's just like a kid who "knows" she won't like the taste of vegetables.

Quaker never ate any waxworms after the first couple of days; I don't know why. Finally, I got sick of discovering dead waxworms at the bottom of the cage and stopped feeding them to her. Perhaps because she wasn't getting enough protein, she started having trouble keeping her feathers. Bulbuls are known to have a long, ugly molting period—but when Quaker molted, she seemed to stay bald for months. Remember how I said Quaker looked sort of like a miniature eagle when I first saw her? Well, now she looks like a miniature eagle that's mistakenly gone through a vacuum cleaner and also had its head replaced with a Ping-Pong ball and its neck replaced with a Popsicle stick. Her body feathers are all tattered, and her head is *amazingly* small now that it's got only about five feathers. It makes her beak look thirty times too big. Plus, you can completely see Quaker's ears now, which is bad. I don't like thinking about a bird's ears. And her tail feathers look like broom straws.

I'm working on this problem. We're still experimenting with different vitamins; I got a special light for her cage; I put iodine into her water; and I stir stinky, stinky kelp powder into her daily fruit. I've also started offering

her a daily bowl of something called Feast Insectivorous. ("With lots of lovely bugs!" one advertisement says.) Feast Insectivorous looks like granola with dried mealworms in it. In addition to mealworms, it contains dried water flies, dried water *fleas*, dried freshwater shrimp, and dried conchs, whatever they are. They can't be the kind of conch with the huge pink shells, can they? Perhaps they're some other kind of lovely bug. Feast Insectivorous is meant for finches, Pekin robins—whatever *they* are—jays, and mynahs. Bulbuls are related to mynahs, so perhaps one day Quaker will realize that she loves Feast Insectivorous. So far, she mostly just throws the dried insects onto the floor.

For several months Quaker and the little birds got along fine. Then came spring—breeding season—and Quaker went nuts. One morning, one of the canaries had a bloody slash between his shoulders. Unsure what had happened, I put him in a separate cage to heal. But the next morning, another canary had the same slash. Quaker was the only bird with a sharp enough beak to have committed the crime.

I felt terrible. I had never thought a female bird would become this aggressive. Obviously, that was wrong. The only solution was to get another flight cage for the little birds so they'd be safe.

It would have been fairest to catch Quaker and move *her* into the new cage, but she flew too fast to catch. On the other hand, if there's a worse job than trying to catch finches, canaries, and parakeets in a net, one after the other, I hope I never have to do it. I had to reach way into the cage and whoosh the net around so all the birds would swoop in my direction. One of them would generally grab the side of the cage and hold on, and I'd try to bring the net down over it. I had to be superfast but also supergentle. I couldn't let the net hurt the birds. If I managed to trap one bird in the net, the others would start zipping around like maniacs. Sometimes they startled me so that I dropped the net and had to start over.

I was sweating and swearing. It took more than an hour to transfer all the littler birds. I still don't know why none of them escaped. But finally the little birds had their own flight cage and Quaker began her lonely vigil.

She couldn't hurt the other birds, but did she miss the company? At one point I called the pet store where I'd found her to ask for advice. "I'll buy her a companion if you think she should have one," I said.

"You'll never find another bulbul" was the answer.

I put some toys into Quaker's cage, but she wasn't interested. Unlike many pet birds, she didn't care about seeing her reflection in a bird mirror. Then I read online that bulbuls like to perch high up in trees where they can see everything that's going on. They like to stand guard—not to play. So I put in several different kinds of perches and hoped that at least the variety would attract her. It took months before she started venturing onto the new perches, but finally she was able to persuade herself to move around the cage. Now she flies around a lot more. I almost wish there were some enemies she could actually guard against. Do you think houseflies count?

Poor Quaker. It's been frustrating. I think she's used to her life at my house, but she'll certainly never be tame. Maybe her "pet quality" isn't quite zero, but it's not much higher than eight percent. I can read my other birds' body language, but I almost never know what Quaker is feeling. She finally knows who I am, but it took over a year before she stopped panicking when she saw me. And she still practically explodes with fear if someone she doesn't recognize tries to feed her.

Laura is especially bothered by this. She doesn't like birds much to begin with. Quaker's rapid, zigzag flight and sharp beak make her nervous. If she has to feed Quaker when I'm away, she sings a special song she composed to the tune of "Deck the Halls." It goes:

Quaker, Quaker, stay in your cage.
I'm a little bit afraid of you.

I have to confess that I'm also a little bit afraid of Quaker. And sad for her. This isn't the life she was meant to live. But I did learn to love her, and I tell myself that at least she's happier than she was at the pet store.

And I think the iodine is working. Quaker is finally getting back some feathers on her head! Wisps, anyway. Well, not even wisps: the new "plumage" is about the size of the hairs on your arm. She's added two new real feathers, but that doesn't help much when all she had before was four. Her little gray ball of a head actually looks worse dusted with white than it did when she was completely bald. But I think she looks beautiful.

the other birds

I shouldn't call them that. It sounds as if I don't think of them as individuals.

But I've had so many canaries, parakeets, and finches over the years that it's hard to keep them straight. They're all different but in small ways. One parakeet likes to swing; another likes to kiss his reflection in the mirror. One finch likes to take the infertile eggs out of her nest and throw them on the ground; another likes to bury the infertile eggs under a new nest and start over. One canary likes to bathe in the red dish every morning; another likes the white dish better. And except for a few color variations, each different bird looks just like the others of his species. Whenever kids come to visit, I tell them that I'll name a bird after them. When they've left, I can never remember which bird it was. If they come back, I just point at one of the birds at random and say, "That's the one I named after you."

True, one time my Gouldian finches did raise a female baby with an orange head instead of a red or

black one. A mutant! For the most part, though, I can't tell the Gouldians apart. I can distinguish the canaries only by color. They're all the color of lemon or orange sherbet, except for my lone lizard canary; she's a mottled brownish green. Since she's easy to pick out, she has a name: Lizzie.

The rest of them *used* to have names. "Is that Moses?" John asked recently, pointing to a yellow canary who was splashing happily around in his bath.

"Uh . . . sure," I said.

JOB

The blind canary in his own little cage? Yes, I know which one *he* is. His name is Job, because he's had so many troubles. He's the one all the other birds picked on so cruelly until I moved him. As his sight got worse and worse, he stopped moving around the cage. He chose a perch in one corner from which he could creep out for food and water without getting lost. You'd think the other birds would ignore him—he was doing his absolute best to keep out of their way!—but no. They knew there was something the matter with Job, and they took it upon themselves to try and drive him away. They would swoop down and peck him as he ventured out toward his food dish. Even worse, they'd stand on the perch above him, lean over, and pull out his head feathers.

In the wild, this would have made a kind of cruel sense. An injured bird would draw predators' attention to the rest of the flock, so they'd be saving themselves and their babies by forcing the disabled bird to leave. In a cage, there was no place for poor Job to escape to. Job didn't act blind, so it took me a while before I realized what was happening to him. But as soon as I saw him being teased, I put him into his own cage.

His new home is right on top of the big cage, so that Job can hear the same bird sounds he's used to. It's also closer to the light, in case he has any vision left. Most important, everything in Job's cage is always the same. He has a very low perch that he can step on and off of. I made it out of a stick and added clipped clothespins at each end to hold it steady. I put his seeds right in front of him, and his water right next to them. If

I hang a lettuce leaf in the cage—canaries love romaine lettuce—I clip it right next to Job's head. If I'm giving him a spray bath, I always pump the spray bottle a few times so he can hear it before I start spraying him. (He ruffles up his feathers expectantly. Spray baths mean a lot to him now that he can no longer see to bathe in a water dish.) There's a note on his cage telling other people to make sure they follow the same rules with Job. He had such a hard time for so long that I figure he's entitled to a predictable life from now on.

EGGS! WAIT—BABIES!

Both my canaries and my Gouldian finches have raised several clutches of babies. (That's the word for it: a "clutch.") And both species have surprised me by hatching babies when I wasn't expecting it.

I never expected my canaries to breed at all. I couldn't even remember which ones were males and which were females. I'd had them for several years, there weren't any nesting materials in the aviary, and they hadn't shown any signs of "broodiness" (acting as if they wanted to hatch eggs). True, sometimes the females would lay an egg in one of their food dishes. But then they'd usually ignore it.

So when I noticed one of the females sitting on a

dish of seeds, I thought she was sick. You hardly ever see a bird sitting still unless something is wrong. She didn't even move when I gave her an experimental poke—just kept sitting there.

Worried, I lifted her off the dish. Three eggs were nestled in the birdseed. She had never laid three at once, and she had never sat on them. Even *I* now suspected something might be up.

I've never outgrown my impatience about waiting for things to happen. When I was little, I used to dig up the carrots I'd planted to see how they were growing. Then I'd pat them back into the dirt. Once, I planted a maple seed in a flowerpot. When a maple seedling finally sprouted, I asked my dad what would make it grow better.

"Time," Dad said.

"Thyme? You mean like the spice?" I was all ready to run down to my mom's spice box and dig out the jar of thyme.

"No," said Dad. "*Time*. You have to *wait*."

That was not what I wanted to hear. I wanted to take a jar of thyme and mix it with water and make a kind of tea that I could sprinkle on my maple seed. Just ordinary time—who cared about that? I don't remember what happened to my maple seed. But I do know that I don't have a homegrown maple tree anywhere, so I assume I got sick of "time" and went on with my life.

Of course, as a grownup, I know that you *have* to

be patient sometimes. But I'm really only a kid in a grownup costume. I couldn't stand waiting to see if those three canary eggs would hatch. I got to know them better than I had ever known any of my birds. Every day I'd gently push the female off the nest (well, off the bowl of seeds) and check to make sure they were all there. Every few days I'd mist the eggs with water. I had read somewhere that that was a good thing to do. I even "candled them"—held each egg up to the light to see how the chicks were developing. I couldn't really tell. I didn't know what to look for, and the light I used wasn't strong enough to see much. Still, it made me feel like a professional canary breeder.

Canaries sit on their eggs for fourteen days. Toward the end of the incubation period, I was afraid to check on the eggs at all. What if I dropped one and a wobbly little chick came out prematurely? It took every bit of my willpower, but I stayed away from the nest until three days after the eggs had been due to hatch. On the third day, I cautiously peeked in at the nest. I could see something pink and blobby under the canary hen. A canary chick! No, two chicks! No, wait, THREE chicks! No, wait, just two. The third egg had not hatched, and it never did. For a couple of days the chicks used it as a sort of propping-up shelf. Then their parents took the egg from the nest and threw it onto the floor of the cage.

It's hard to convey how, well, ugly a newly hatched

canary chick is. Cute, but ugly. The babies are feather-less and floppy, with a few little puffs of down that somehow look worse than no feathers at all. You can see their ears—just wrinkled holes in their heads. Their eyes are like tiny gray jellybeans sealed under a thin layer of skin; their wings, like pink toothpicks bent in half. Their heads wobble on necks that look so frail you can hardly believe the heads don't just fall off. Yet every time their parents leave or return to the nest, those heavy heads shoot straight up into the air, and their beaks gape wide open. They are eating machines.

Right under a canary chick's beak is a little food-holding sac called the crop. When the crop is full of food, it looks like two tiny, transparent bags crammed with disgusting, yellow, seed-filled vomit. Which is basi-cally what it is. All day long, over and over, the parent birds swallow food and regurgitate it into each baby's beak until the crop is filled.

I hate that word—"regurgitate"—don't you? It always reminds me of a chant we used to shout when I was a kid.

Regurgitate! Regurgitate!
Throw up all the food you ate!
V-O-M-I-T! VOMIT! Ugh.

But regurgitation is what's going on if the parent birds are doing their jobs. Checking to see if a chick's crop is full is the best way to tell how it's doing in the early days. Fortunately, you don't have to look too hard. Until it's covered with feathers, a full crop is *much* too visible.

The chicks won't look like what we think of as baby birds until they're about a week old. But they grow so fast that every time you look at them, you notice something different. For the first few days, they're visibly bigger in the afternoon than they were in the morning. For the first ten days, they double in weight *every day*. Imagine what you'd look like if your weight doubled every day!

The chicks' wing feathers are the first to emerge. They come out like a row of little spikes along the birds' skinny arms. I suppose that's because wing feathers are the most useful in times of danger, although of course it's not as if a chick could fly with them at this stage. After about eight days, the chicks are armored in stiff little pinfeathers. Their eyes are slitted open, making them look like lizards. ("Dinosaurs with beaks," a friend of mine once called baby birds.) They're so big now, and they can stretch their necks so high, that the parents really have to work to get food into each baby's beak. The others are weaving around like basketball players, trying to intercept every bite meant for someone else. Sometimes a parent will have to scramble up onto the shoulders of one of the babies in order to feed another.

Meanwhile, the whole clutch is squealing, each trying to outscream the others. For baby birds, getting their parents to notice them is the main job. I have so much trouble distinguishing my *adult* birds that I never understand how the parent canaries can tell which baby they've fed already. This is where a smaller or weaker chick would have trouble: if she can't make enough noise or reach her head as high as those of her brothers and sisters, the parents may not notice her at all. Luckily, my canaries have never had that problem.

A couple of days later, the babies start to stretch their wings. On hot days, they like to hang their heads over the side of the nest. At this point their mom stops sleeping on the nest; she just can't cover them with her body anymore, and they're kicking and shoving too much for her to get a good night's sleep. The chicks' skin must be tougher than it looks. They're now so active that they walk all over each other—even standing on each others' heads sometimes—but their claws never seem to leave scratches. By this point, they "only" need to be fed four times a day, and they're as big as their parents.

At sixteen days, it's impossible to understand how the babies can stay in the nest without pushing each other out. They bounce all over the place. They jump into the air and flap their wings like dogs shaking off water. They hop up onto the nest's edge and peek over, calculating what would happen if they jumped. They shove one another out of the way when it's time to eat. If I were a mother canary, this is when I would be *totally* sick of my babies. Fortunately, they're just about to be able to fly. Unfortunately, they'll still need to be fed for a few days after they've left the nest. Fortunately, they don't need as much food by then. Unfortunately, they're all over the cage, so the parents have to work harder.

After my first clutch of canary babies hatched, I made sure to take any more eggs out of the seed dishes. I didn't want the females to be too stressed out laying eggs, and I didn't want a billion canaries. But I kept all the babies, who are much tamer than their parents. If you come to visit, I'll name one of them after you.

WAIT—GOULDIAN BABIES!

In the case of my Gouldian finches, I was hoping they'd breed. But I didn't expect much.

Gouldians are the most beautiful finches I've ever

seen. They come in all kinds of colors. The commonest is still pretty fancy: a bright fern green with a red or a black head outlined in turquoise, a yellow stomach, and a purple bib on the chest. But Gouldians are known not to be very good parents. They make sloppy nests, for one thing. Once, a Gouldian female of mine laid her eggs on the floor of her nesting box, then arranged exactly two pieces of grass on top of them. *That's* not going to get anything hatched.

Unlike canaries, Gouldians like privacy for raising their babies—or their imaginary babies. The nesting boxes I order for the flight cage have a deep, cozy back chamber for the nest, and a front chamber for a "porch."

I got my first nesting box well before the breeding season was supposed to start. That, I hoped, would help the finches get used to it. As soon as I put in the first nesting box, my Gouldian pair rushed over to it. Standing on its roof, they both peeked inside the porch. Then the male timidly hopped onto the porch and peeked inside the nesting chamber. After a second, the female joined him. There followed a long time of cheeping, rustling, turning their little heads this way and that, hopping up onto the porch perch and hopping down, flying back to the roof and peeking inside again. You could tell how interested and curious they were, but you couldn't tell whether they had any idea what the box was for.

It was still weeks until spring, so they had a long time to get used to the idea of having babies. When it was finally June and I saw the male jumping up and down in front of the female, I was pretty sure things were going in the right direction.

Lots of birds have courtship routines. If you're ever in a place with a lot of pigeons, watch how the males puff up their neck feathers and trot around after the females as if they're trying to get the females to an important meeting on time. (The females generally seem to ignore them, though they do start walking a little faster.) You're not likely to be in a place with a lot of whooping cranes, but someday you should try to watch their courtship dance. They flap their huge wings and kick their long, stiltlike legs and bow and whirl around—and whoop, of course.

The way male Gouldian finches court their mates is to jump up and down. They look like little eager windup toys as they hop on their straight little legs. We probably wouldn't be too interested in humans who did this—at least, not interested enough to marry them—but it works with female finches. Many, many times my male finch built nests out of hay I put into the cage for them. Many, many times the female laid eggs in the nest and sat on them for two weeks. And many, many times those eggs didn't hatch, and the male would just build

another nest on top of the old eggs. When I cleaned out the nesting box at the end of the breeding season, it was full of old eggs and old nests.

Finally, I got sick of this. I stopped putting hay and straw into the aviary. I left the nesting box in the cage, but didn't check it. "Stop thinking about eggs," I told myself. I knew the finches would lay them from time to time; they might even sit on them for a couple of weeks. But nothing would come of it. If I wanted more Gouldians, I would have to buy more from a breeder.

Six months later, I was cleaning the prairie dog's cage when I heard a faint cheeping coming from the birdcage. That's a new sound, I thought, and forgot about it. The next day, though, I heard it again—a tiny bit louder this time.

There's no mistaking the sound of new baby birds—a tiny, insistent cheep that's as regular as a pulse. Carefully I raised the lid of the nesting box. The female finch scooted out of the way, and I saw two minuscule babies sitting in a nest made of newspaper. Their dad must have made it by tearing off strips of paper from the bottom of the cage. And I hadn't even noticed!

Well, I thought, if they did all this when I was ignoring them, I'll just keep on ignoring them and see what happens.

And it worked! Maybe the secret was that I left them alone. Maybe it was "time," as my dad had told me when I was little. In any case, the two babies survived, and their parents raised three babies the following year.

I've got a new female Gouldian finch now. She's a yellowback—yellow all over except for her purple "bib" and an orange head. Since she's easy to recognize, I've even given her a name: Five. I'm going to let Five get used to the other finches for a year, and then I'm putting in the nesting box again.

I can't wait to see what colors the babies will be.

HOW TO CUT A RABBIT'S NAILS IN
THIRTEEN IMPOSSIBLE STEPS

1. Notice that all three of your rabbits have toenails that look like a child's drawing of a bear's claws. Don't do anything for a couple of days. Maybe the nails will wear down on their own.

2. Watch the special rabbit-toenail-cutting video you ordered online from the House Rabbit Association. Notice how easy they make it look, and how relaxed and well behaved their rabbits are. Maybe your own rabbits should watch the video so they can learn to behave!

3. Remember that one of the things the video tells you is to get your rabbits used to being picked up every day. Remember, too, that you haven't done this since the last time you cut the rabbits' toenails, because the rabbits hate it so much. Once again, you will have to chase your rabbits instead of calmly picking them up like the well-trained rabbit owners in the video.

4. Stall for a while by getting the "clipping area" ready. Place a soft towel on a table so the rabbits will feel safe and secure. Have the nail clippers handy, along with some paper towels and a little jar of styptic powder. The powder is to be used if you clip the nails too short

and they start to bleed. (Which *always* happens.)

Well, that's enough work for one day!

5. Watch the video again, admiring the way the narrator fits the clippers gently around the rabbits' toenails and says "Press . . . press . . . clip." You're supposed to press the clippers before clipping, you see. That way, if you're clipping the nail too high, the rabbit will let you know it hurts *before* you actually cut the nail. It

would be a lot easier if you could give the rabbits their manicure in front of the VCR, but that would mean cutting their nails on the kitchen counter. Your dogs would be way too interested and would keep trying to jump up and sniff the rabbits, which would cause all kinds of trouble. But if you were to shut the dogs out of the kitchen, they would bark and distract you from your important task. So all you can do is try to memorize the video.

6. When you know the video by heart, it's time to visit the rabbits. Start with Stumper. He's the easiest, because he has only three legs. Five fewer nails to cut! Unfortunately, Stumper sheds more than any of the other rabbits, and prob-ably more than any other rabbit in the world. When you pick him up, bushels of rabbit hair fly off into your face.

7. Realize you have forgotten everything in the video except for the part where you're supposed to say "Press . . . press . . . clip." To get to that point, you need to have the rabbit in position. Loudly call, "Hey, someone get in here and help me hold Stumper!" After eight minutes, one of your kids wanders in.

8. As the two of you are trying to get Stumper into position, he suddenly closes his eyes and slumps over onto his side. His breathing is shallow and rapid. Can a rabbit faint? He's not faking it, is he?

9. Decide Stumper is too stressed out for this. Return him to his pen.

10. Decide that Mojo can have his nails clipped when you take him to the rabbit vet next week to have his teeth checked.

12. Decide that Crosby's nails are probably okay for one more day.

13. Resolve to start again tomorrow, when you'll all be in a better mood.

P. S. To cut your dog's toenails, have one person hold the dog while another person holds a chicken drumstick just out of reach. While the dog strains and struggles to bite the drumstick, the person holding the dog can quickly clip off a few nails. As soon as the dog notices what's going on, give him or her a little piece of chicken; then start the whole process over. Or just have the vet do it the next time the dog has a checkup.

rein, plumpy, and frowny

I knew I couldn't write this book without getting one more animal. A nonfiction story needs to be up-to-date, doesn't it? I didn't want to talk about a lot of pets I *used* to have. That would disappoint you, and I would never want to disappoint my dear, darling readers, would I?

No, no! I *owed* it to you to get a new animal. That way, when you wanted to persuade your parents that you deserved a pet of your own, you'd be able to say things like "Ann Hodgman has a *wallaby*. Why won't you let me get a little, tiny gerbil?"

So I started to poke around online. Almost immediately I realized that you can buy pretty much any kind of exotic animal if you're an adult and you're willing to pay enough.

I could have bought a baby woodchuck. A baby raccoon. A baby capybara. (Look it up.) Baby chipmunks, baby opossums, baby antelope, baby marmosets. (Look it up. I bet you haven't put the dictionary away.

You haven't even taken it off the shelf, have you?) Baby wolves, even. Think how exciting it would be to bottle-feed a baby wolf!

BUT! BUT! BUT! . . .

. . . Think what a mess I'd be in when that wolf was an adult, without enough space and without enough to do and without other wolves to teach it how to live the way a wolf should.

It wouldn't have mattered how much I loved a wolf cub, or how cool it would be to own one. I couldn't give it the right kind of home. And when you think about it, that's true of most of the exotic animals you can manage to acquire for yourself if you try hard enough.

Take a chipmunk, for example. I have to say I always feel a little jolt of excitement when I realize I could actu-ally buy a chipmunk. Imagine all that cuteness right up close where I could see it and pick it up and hand-feed it peanuts! Why, it would be a million times cuter than a plain old hamster!

But could a chipmunk be a real pet? And would it enjoy being a pet?

Just because an animal has been born in captivity doesn't mean it's a domestic animal. I've loved my sugar gliders and my prairie dogs, and I think they've probably liked me—especially the prairie dogs. I've done my best to give both species a good life.

But I've never been sure that prairie dogs and sugar gliders were meant to be confined. Even the happiest caged prairie dog will chew the bars of its cage a lot of the time. That's not normal animal behavior. Even the happiest pet sugar glider will spend most of the night trying to get out of its cage. That proves it should never have been in there in the first place.

I found several exotic-animal breeders who sell baby raccoons online. A raccoon is another animal I've dreamed about owning ever since I was little. But here's some information from the "tip sheet" one breeder passes out if you're thinking about buying one of their babies:

- Rarely does a raccoon make a good pet.

- A raccoon can and will bite. Make sure you have a liability insurance policy to protect you if your raccoon does bite and scratch someone.

- Roundworm is a serious problem for raccoons. . . . It can be transferred to humans and other pets. This can cause blindness, central nervous system damage, and death!

- Raccoons are notoriously messy diners. They mix their food with their water and end up with a big soupy mess every time.

- Raccoons can be litter-box trained, though once they are trained they will still express anger or displeasure by eliminating on something of yours.

Sounds great, doesn't it? And this is from a company that *sells raccoons*. What would they write if they were trying to *discourage* you from buying one?

Of course, they don't have any pictures of adult raccoon pets on their Web site. They only show tiny, adorable babies eating Cheerios and playing with a rubber ducky. After all, they want your money—and they know you can't return a raccoon like a pair of pants that doesn't fit.

You see my point. Even for you, my dear, darling readers, it wouldn't have been worth it to add a really "interesting" animal to my lineup. I was stuck with the same possibilities that face *you*. Rabbits, gerbils, hamsters, some kind of uncomplicated lizard, guinea pigs . . .

Guinea pigs! I hadn't owned a guinea pig since fourth grade, and Laura had always longed for one. The guinea pigs at her preschool—a mother and daughter named Lovie and Baby—were her favorite thing there. Her teachers allowed the kids to carry Baby and Lovie wrapped in towels, and Laura was always lugging one or the other around the classroom. I let her take care of Baby and Lovie during the summer between three-year-old and four-year-old preschool, and she had a great time with them. *I* didn't have such a great time, because the guinea pigs were in a way-too-small cage that I had to clean every day. Back then, cage-cleaning still bothered me; besides, John was only six months old that summer, and I felt as though I moved from diaper changing to cage changing without ever stopping. Anyway, Laura won the "Best with Guinea Pigs" award at the end of preschool, and she still has the medal hanging on her mirror.

As the years went by and I added more and more animals to the household, Laura could never understand why I didn't want a guinea pig. "Especially when they're so much cuter than rabbits," she once said (incorrectly).

"But they're so messy," I objected.

"Not worse than rabbits," she said.

"But I already *have* rabbits!"

"Then a cute little guinea pig or two won't make any difference," said Laura.

So I started thinking about it for this book. Maybe I could get that new kind of hairless guinea pig that looks so alien and weird! "Skinny pigs," they're called. They have a little bit of fuzz on their heads, but the rest of their body is smooth and hairless, like suede. Their skin is sensitive and they get cold easily—not too surprising—but I thought that wouldn't be too hard to take care of. "I can just put some fleece blankets in their pen," I thought. "It won't be hard to wash the blankets." (Every single day, day after day after day after day.) The babies are expensive, but it would be worth it. . . .

And then my conscience kicked in *again*. I promise that this bossy part of the chapter won't last much longer, but I have to give you another little lecture even if you've already heard it before.

ANOTHER LITTLE LECTURE

Everyone likes to start out with a cute baby animal. That's why pet stores sell as many babies as they can. But what happens to the ones they don't sell? You don't want to know. And what happens to all those babies once they grow up? Lots of people lose interest in them then. Thousands and thousands of guinea pigs—and other pets, of course—are abandoned every year just because they're not as cute as they used to be. How could I buy a cute baby when there were so many adult guinea pigs looking for homes?

Reluctantly, I decided I had to get a rescue guinea pig, one I adopted from someone who takes in abandoned pets. Most likely, that would mean an adult animal. Possibly, it would mean the guinea pig wasn't particularly tame: being abandoned doesn't do a lot for an animal's friendliness. But I was confident that I'd come to think my guinea pigs were cute no matter how old they were.

And I knew that since guinea pigs *are* domestic animals, I'd be able to tame even the shyest pig after a while. In some ways, it might even be more fun to start out with a guinea pig who was afraid of me! That way, every step toward getting her to trust me would be a real accomplishment.

So I looked around for a few weeks, and I found Cindy.

My friend Cindy is an animal rescuer who lives about an hour from my house. For several years now, she has worked to place abandoned guinea pigs or to find sponsors for her "special needs" pigs. (My favorite of these is Minerva, who was born without eyes. I begged to adopt her, but Cindy said no. She said, "I would never place an animal that had this kind of health issue. There might be other things wrong with Minerva down the line.") Most of the time, Cindy has a dozen or so adoptable guinea pigs. She posts their pictures and descriptions on Petfinder.com, so you can do your own comparison shopping online. That's how I found Rein.

REIN

I wasn't much interested in Rein at first. Her photo was dreadful; she looked like a scared, flattened-out rat with glaring red eyes. And I'd been looking for a bonded pair of guinea pigs, not just one. Guinea pigs are such sociable animals that they really shouldn't be alone. I know a vet who started out with a single guinea pig when she was a little girl. Soon she got a second one, to keep the first one company. Two years later, the first one died, so she got a third one to keep the second one company. She's kept this up for *twenty-eight years*.

"Get Rein *and* another pair!" suggested my friend Molly. But I just laughed her off. Two guinea pigs were the most I could handle.

Still, Rein's story was so sad that I couldn't stop thinking about it. She had been found abandoned in the basement of an apartment complex. Running around loose and starving in a dark basement! It was no wonder that, as Cindy wrote, "This poor girl is petrified and will need a lot of handling and reassurance."

I asked Cindy if I could adopt Rein with another pig. But Cindy didn't think Rein would be able to make friends. "I put her in with Minerva," she wrote, "and Rein went after her. And she meant business. I had to hold her back with one hand and grab Minerva with the other." Since Minerva was both blind and young, she couldn't possibly have been a threat to Rein. Most likely, Cindy thought, Rein had been too abused and scared ever to be able to live with a companion.

Well. Here I was lecturing you guys about how you should adopt an animal that needs a home. And here was Rein, an ugly guinea pig who would probably never be that friendly and who no one else would want to adopt. . . .

You should see Rein now.

She's turned into a beautiful, glossy, plump girl. Maybe a little *too* plump—she's shaped like an eggplant. John calls her "the water balloon." When Rein stands still, her body settles down around her feet like an inner tube. She lies down to eat. We don't care; we love her that way. Rein doesn't enjoy being picked up, but she'll stand there dreamily with her eyes closed while you scratch her head and ears. She keeps up a constant flow of chatter when you're nearby. "Just

reminding you I'm here," she's saying, "and if you have a second, could you get me some more lettuce?"

In addition to being fed and being patted, Rein loves her Cuddle Cup. ("I hate that name," my husband says. I myself like to say "Cuddle Cup" as often as I can. Cuddle Cup. Cuddle Cup.) This is a sort of pouch lined with soft fluff. Since Rein likes to use her Cuddle Cup as both a bed and a toilet, I line it with squares of cloth I've cut from an old pair of red sweatpants. Once, I took the sweatpant square out and put in a paper towel lining instead. Rein *hated* the sight of all that scary white. She wouldn't go in the Cuddle Cup at all. Back in went the sweatpant squares, and then she snuggled down again.

Recently, I've been working to persuade Rein that green squares from an old sweater are also acceptable. (That way, I don't have to do laundry as often.) She was upset at first, but there are signs that she will come around to this point of view.

PLUMPY

In the pen right next to Rein's are two more guinea pigs, Plumpy and Frowny. How did they get there? Why do I have three guinea pigs when for so long I never even wanted one? I'm not quite sure.

I still thought I could find a friend to put in Rein's pen, so I asked Cindy if she had any guinea pigs she thought might be suitable. I was hoping for a guinea pig with "rosettes"—those curly swirls of fur that I always think look so funny.

"Are you fussy about color?" Cindy wrote back. "I just got three six-week-old females in. One of the worst cases of neglect I have seen. They are white with pink eyes (the ones that everyone dislikes). They have rosettes, though!"

To tell the truth, I wasn't so attracted to albino animals. But that's the wrong way to feel. An animal's color doesn't matter any more than a person's does. And once again, Plumpy's story was hard to turn my back on.

Plumpy's mother had starved to death while nursing Plumpy and her sisters. Their owner hadn't realized that mother guinea pigs need extra food or that babies need solid food even while they're nursing. So the babies had tried and tried to get milk from their mom, and finally the stress on her body had killed her. Only then did it occur to their owner that something might be wrong.

All three babies were scrawny and weak. Cindy wasn't sure they would survive. But she crammed their cage with food, and in a few days they started to recover.

"Last night Plumpy was so cute when I gave her her bedtime snack," Cindy e-mailed me a few days later. "She couldn't make up her mind if she wanted to eat, to race around her cage, or to popcorn." Popcorning is the word for the up-and-down leaps guinea pigs make when they're excited.

"It is a joy and a sadness to watch these three babies," Cindy went on. "When they are fed, their eyes light up like neon; they don't know what to do first or what to eat first. They're so excited that they actually have food that they'll popcorn while they're eating. I wonder if they will ever relax and realize that food will always be there for them."

When I first brought Plumpy home, she was so worried about her food that she would try to hide it before she ate it. Now she's a big strong girl with curly white fur, though I don't think she'll ever actually become plump. (Laura insisted on naming her Plumpy no matter how skinny she was.) I also don't know if she'll ever like being touched—and she's a biter, so I have to be careful around her. But recently she began to let me tap her on the nose. Progress! Maybe one day she'll enjoy being patted. In the meantime, she has Frowny to snuggle with.

FROWNY

Sometimes you can help animals become friends if you introduce them in a "neutral space"—a place neither of them has ever been before. This keeps either animal from thinking, "Get out of my territory!"

A good neutral space is a bathtub—empty, of course. You line the tub with newspaper for easy cleanup, place the two animals into it, and wait for the explosion. At least, an explosion is what happened when I put Rein and Plumpy together. Standing there in the tub, Rein ground her teeth and shook all over. Then she made a sudden dash at Plumpy. And, as Cindy had predicted, Rein meant business. This wasn't some kind of "let's shyly sniff each other's noses to get acquainted." This was "I'll GET you!"

Hastily I scooped up both pigs and returned them to their own pens. Rein was still chattering and shaking with rage. Plumpy didn't realize anything had happened. But now I had a new problem. Rein obviously didn't care whether she had a friend—but Plumpy was going to be lonely without a cagemate. So back I went to Cindy's house. And there was six-week-old Frowny waiting for me.

That's another bonus about adopting, by the way. Peoples' pets are always having babies that they can't find homes for, so if you wait long enough, you can usually find a baby to adopt. You don't *always* have to get an adult animal.

Frowny is a brown and white female with a little puff of fur between her eyes that makes her look angry all the time. She's actually very sweet, but boy, is she shy. She almost never comes out into the open when we're nearby; she just huddles in her pigloo, peeking out occasionally to see if we've gone. (A pigloo is a round, plastic house that looks like—yes!—an igloo. Like Cuddle Cup, it's another name that my husband can't stand.) There's no question of her letting me touch her for the time being. Right now I'm working on training her to take food from my hand.

The other two pigs have learned to eat from my

hand. Show either of them a carrot, and they'll grab it and wave it around triumphantly like a big cigar. Then they'll rush off to find a place to eat it in secret.

I let Frowny hear them crunching away for a minute. She darts over to Plumpy, hoping to steal Plumpy's carrot. Plumpy whirls it out of reach, still crunching. Frowny looks up at me, clearly hoping I'll drop a carrot for her. Instead, I hold it out toward her. Frowny all but stamps with frustration: why won't I let her have her stupid carrot? Slowly, slowly she creeps toward my hand. She sniffs the carrot, pulls back, sniffs, pulls back. I move it toward her, and she runs away.

"Okay," I say, "I guess you don't want it. I'll give it to one of the rabbits." Straightening up, I act as if I'm going to walk away.

Frowny dashes frantically around the pen. I hold out the carrot again, and this time she takes it.

Patience isn't one of my strengths, but I have no choice around the guinea pigs. You can't rush them. Once, when Rein's eyes were closed while I patted her nose, I tried to pick her up. She screamed like a train whistle, and it took a week before she would even let me touch her again. Now, finally, she lets us hold her wrapped up in a towel. She'll even sometimes go to sleep in our laps. Then she wakes up and seems to say, "Oh, my God, what am I doing here? Put me BACK! Put me BACK!" But she really is getting tamer every day.

In the few months since the guinea pigs have come to live with us, we're all much happier. I know I've given three abandoned pets a home, which makes me feel like a rescuing angel. More important, I've realized that you really can make yourself love an animal just by working at it. I never used to care about guinea pigs. Now I can't imagine living without them.

I'll never agree with Laura that guinea pigs are cuter than rabbits. But I will say they're *almost* as cute.

some kind of friend
for stumper

"Okay. Okay. I'm really going to start today. I'm going to bond Stumper with Mojo and Crosby."

This is what I told myself for weeks.

As I told you before, Stumper has been so lonely ever since his companion, Blink, died. He's desperate for attention. When I walk past his pen, he rushes up

and presses his kind donkey face against the bars to get a pat. As often as I can, I pat him and scratch his ears for him. I'll even clean out the earwax in his left ear—the one he can't scratch because he's missing his left hind leg.

Do you want to know the weirdest thing about Stumper's earwax? No, it's too weird. I can't tell you about it.

Well, okay.

No, wait, maybe I really shouldn't tell you.

Well, okay, I will.

Whenever a rabbit scratches the inside of his ears, he always licks his foot afterward. So when I started scratching Stumper's ears for him, it occurred to me to offer my earwax-y finger to him. And he eagerly licked off the wax.

Gross, right? But there has to be a reason for it. I wrote to a rabbit newsgroup asking if any other rabbit owners had ever noticed that their rabbits ate their own earwax.

One woman wrote snottily, "I give my rabbit *real* treats, like carrots. I don't make him eat wax!"

But another, much smarter woman who works with a rabbit vet told me, "Whenever we clean a rabbit's ears, we always let him lick the cotton swab with the wax on it. We think it's a source of vitamin D."

Take *that*, stupid other woman who only gives her rabbit carrots!

Still, even sticking my finger way down into Stumper's ear doesn't make me as much fun as another rabbit would be. I can let Stumps out of his pen and play games with him, but I can't do it as well as Blink could. I'm certainly not going to crawl inside his cardboard play tube and jump out at him the way Blink used to. (I'd get stuck.) And I can't spend hours lying on the floor with him, either. For all of these things, another rabbit would be best.

But everything about a rabbit is more complicated than most people realize.

UNDERSTANDING RABBITS, OR TRYING TO

Whenever people meet all my pets, someone is sure to ask how smart one of them is. This question doesn't make sense. All species are *very* smart at being themselves. If someone suddenly turned you into a snail, you wouldn't be nearly as smart about being a snail as a real snail is. So people who say that rabbits aren't intelligent don't know what they're talking about.

In pet terms, though, it may surprise you to learn that rabbits are just about as smart as cats and dogs. Like cats and dogs, they need a lot of space to roam around and plenty of interesting activities. So why don't they behave more like cats and dogs? Why aren't they friendlier? The difference is that they're prey animals. In the wild, rabbits would be *eaten* by animals like cats and dogs. Their brains and bodies and habits are all designed for escaping predators—which includes people.

Rabbits don't usually like being picked up and carried around. It makes them think they're being attacked. They don't even like it if you swoop down too fast to pat them.

They're most active during dawn and dusk, when most predators would be sleeping. During the day, they mostly like to sit around.

Sometimes the way a rabbit shows that it likes you is by ignoring you. That can be hard to understand for a person who's used to dogs and cats. But rabbits are used to running away from larger animals instinctively. If a rabbit ignores you, it means he trusts you.

People are used to the way cats and dogs behave. Dogs and cats have been domesticated for thousands of years and bred to react to people in certain ways. (Rabbits have been domesticated for only about five centuries.) Dogs more than cats, of course; you can usually tell what a dog wants and what it's thinking, whereas cats are sometimes harder to read. Still, any cat owner eventually gets to know what her cat is feeling.

With a rabbit, it's all different. Rabbits' faces aren't as expressive as those of cats and dogs. That's partly because their eyes are on the sides of their heads so they can spot predators more easily. It's partly because humans haven't spent centuries trying to breed rabbits to be better companions. Whatever the reason, it's hard to read a rabbit's expression by looking at his face.

A rabbit's body language is also hard for people to understand. When a rabbit is really relaxed and happy, it will sometimes throw itself onto the ground and lie there motionless for a few seconds, as if it were dead. A startling thing to see until you get used to it.

Since it's hard for people to understand rabbits, they sometimes think it's all right for rabbits to be left alone. Wrong, wrong, wrong! Like cats and dogs, rabbits get bored and lonely without company. Like cats and dogs, they should live inside the house with their owners, and not be caged up. Nothing makes me sadder than to see a rabbit being kept outside in a hutch by itself. "He's fine," his owners will say. "Rabbits can handle any kind of weather." Even if that were true (and it isn't), they can't handle being by themselves. A rabbit alone outside is scared and lonely. Even though rabbits chew things like baseboards and table legs, and even though their hay and their fur get all over the place, and even though they can only be *sort* of housebroken, rabbits should be house pets. And in addition to humans, they should have other rabbits for company.

If you've always dreamed about owning a rabbit, and this discourages you, good! Getting a rabbit is not like getting a hamster. A rabbit is just as big a responsibility as a cat or a dog, and it can live for just as long. If you want a rabbit, you need to be prepared for what it means to take care of one.

I learned all this the hard way—by making mistakes that are too sad to tell you about. And I vowed that the rabbits who live with me now will get the best care I can give them. My rabbits live in pens on the floor that are about nine by twelve feet, and every day they get a long time to run around loose and hang out with us.

SO WHAT TO DO ABOUT STUMPER?

I can't just pick him up and plunk him down in Mojo and Crosby's pen and say, "Here you go, guys! A new friend!" *Another* complicated thing about rabbits is that they don't bond very easily. Mojo is tiny, but he bullies Stumper any chance he gets. One of his favorite activities is standing outside Stumper's pen "guarding" him. When Stumper was having some free time, Mojo once actually jumped out of his own pen—I still don't know how—ran up to Stumper, and started beating him up. When I let Mojo and Crosby out for floor time, I have to be sure Stumper's pen is barricaded, or Mojo would bite him through the bars of the pen.

Poor Stumps is too much of a goofball to understand why Mojo doesn't like him. He never fights back. Maybe that's because he's not very nimble on his three legs, but I think it's even more because he gets confused. He's such a nice doofus that he can't understand a mean rabbit. What's this little guy trying to do to him? Why is this happening? Shaking, Stumper turns and blunders his way into his cardboard tube to recover. Mojo hops off to explore, satisfied that he's put Stumper in his place for one more day.

Still, rabbits need other rabbits. And all the bunny experts say that the best way to introduce two enemy rabbits is to take them for a car ride together.

The thinking is that rabbits hate the car—hate the noise and the vibrations. So if you put them into a crate together and drive them around for a few minutes every day, they'll be too scared to fight. They'll huddle together for comfort and gradually get to know each other. Once you've driven them around for a couple of weeks, you can put them together for a few minutes each day in some kind of unfamiliar space: an empty bathtub or a room where neither of them has ever been. They may be nervous at first, but they'll recognize each other from sharing those terrible car rides. After a few days, they'll be friends.

Or that's what the experts say. But the experts have never met Mojo, with his sinister ways. I've tried crating him with Stumper, and I couldn't even *get* them to the car. Mojo flies into a rage immediately. He hurls himself onto Stumper and sinks his mean little teeth into Stumper's back.

By the way, I love Mojo. The brown markings around his eyes look like little eyeglasses. And he's as sweet as pie when he's alone or with Crosby. It's only Stumper who brings out the evil in him. I'm supposed to spray the two rabbits with water if they start to fight, but it hardly seems fair to spray Stumper when he's just standing there trying not to be bitten.

So what I always end up doing is immediately returning each rabbit to his own pen. Mojo proudly tells Crosby, "I beat up that sucker again." Stumper runs into his cardboard tube to recover.

A rabbit expert would say this is all my fault for not being patient enough, that I should wait longer before giving up. Sometimes it can take months before two rabbits become friends.

Months! I'm not putting Stumper through this for months! In fact, the only reason I tried the crate thing more than *twice* was that I wanted a happy ending for this chapter.

But I've finally decided that the happy ending won't be Stumper moving in with Mojo and Crosby. It also won't be me adopting another rabbit to be Stumper's friend. Three rabbits are plenty for now. Stumper is going to have to be bonded with Rein.

STUMPER AND REIN

Though Rein is also as sweet as pie, she'll probably never learn to like my two other guinea pigs, Plumpy and Frowny. I had thought Rein would just have to be friends with the humans in the house, but then I began to wonder if she and Stumper might get along.

Again, I'm fighting the experts on this. Rabbits are supposed to be dangerous to guinea pigs. They rarely fight, but an accidental kick from a rabbit's powerful hind leg could kill a guinea pig.

But Stumper only has one hind leg, so he couldn't kick all that hard. Besides, he doesn't seem like the kick-y type of rabbit! And wouldn't a guinea pig be a better companion than no one? Of course she would.

When Laura and I put Rein into Stumper's pen to see what they'd do, they didn't fight or even scuffle. They just stood there, staring at each other. We put in a pile of lettuce, and they shared it for a couple of minutes. Then, as usual, Stumper ran into his cardboard tube to recover.

But at least neither of them had done any biting or bullying. So I came up with a new plan.

I've moved Rein's large pen inside Stumper's much larger one. For now, they can see each other through the bars of Rein's pen and exchange sniffs.

Every day I give them their greens side by side. That way, they're close to each other while they're enjoying their favorite activity.

And every day I leave the door of Rein's pen open for a bit so that the two animals can visit each other if they want to. So far, Rein hasn't ventured outside her pen. But Stumper has come to visit her a couple of times. He sniffed around the borders of her pen, sampled the pellets in her bowl, and looked with interest at the two guinea pigs in the pen next door.

Rein's not delighted about these visits. She follows Stumper around in a worried way, like a grandma following a toddler. Every now and then, she dashes into her pigloo to de-stress. Stumper thinks this is a game, and rushes after her—but he can't get even his head into her pigloo.

The one thing Rein will never give Stumper is snuggling time. Rabbits spend a lot of their day licking and cuddling each other. Guinea pigs don't do that. I've seen Stumper thrust his head toward Rein, asking her to nuzzle him. Unlike a rabbit, Rein doesn't understand what Stumpy means. She either darts away or nips him. So I have to make up the snuggling opportunities myself. I make sure to brush Stumper often and to stroke his nose for five minutes a day. And to clean his ear, of course.

I think that as long as I give each animal plenty of hiding places, they should be okay. I'll leave Rein's pen open for an hour a day . . . then two hours . . . and so on until I can leave it open all the time. If she wants privacy, she'll be able to hide in her pigloo or her little wooden tent. If Stumpy wants privacy, he'll be able to hide in his cardboard tunnel or jump up into his haybox. And if either of them wants company, a friend will be right there.

I'll let you know how it turns out.

snappingy

I never thought I'd have a big tank of worms on my kitchen counter, but that was before Snappingy came along. Snapping turtles eat worms, you see.

You can get them to eat other foods: chicken and shrimp and *dried* shrimp and dried krill, which you can shake into the tank from a little carton that looks like a saltshaker. And they eat mealworms and the occasional piece of roast beef. And in the wild, when they're big enough, they eat the occasional finger or axe handle, or at least bite them in half. But lots of turtle experts say that worms are the best food for snapping turtles. And Snappingy has to have the best, because he is the best baby snapping turtle the world has ever known, even though he *is* covered with algae.

So, when Snappingy had grown big enough to eat them, I ordered a hundred red worms from a place called Worm Man's Worm Farm. They looked just like regular earthworms, the kind you find all over the side-walk after it rains (and sometimes can't help riding your bike over). And I took such good care of them—feeding them old bits of lettuce and hay and special worm chow—that soon we had more like a million red worms. I'd originally kept them in an old plastic cake box; now I had to move them to a huge plastic bin. Once a day or so, I would dig around in their compost, spot a likely candidate, and pull it out with my fingers.

The experience gave me a new respect for robins. Worms pull back much harder than you'd expect; just when you think you have one for sure, it slides out of your fingers and disappears underground. Of course robins have beaks, which are pinchier than fingers. To imitate a beak, David dug Snappingy's worms out with a tiny pickle fork. But I couldn't bear the thought of stabbing them by accident, so I kept using my fingers.

"Why don't you name the worms, if you care about

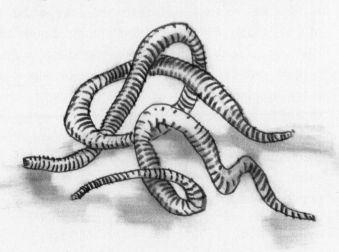

them so much?" David suggested. "They could be Wormingy, Squirmingy, Wigglingy . . ."

He was kidding, of course, but the last thing I needed to do was think even *more* about the worms. It was bad enough that I felt sorry for them when I fed them to Snappingy; it would be *way* worse if I thought of them as individuals. As gross as they were, some of them had too much personality already. When I'd drop them into Snappingy's tank, they would tie themselves into actual knots. A few were smart enough—if "smart" is the word I want; maybe what I mean is "desperate"— to climb out of the water and creep up to the top of the tank. I always felt sorry for them then, and put them back into their worm box to recover. Of course that only meant I'd be feeding them to Snappingy later, but I wanted to give them a break.

The worm's bin was next to our microwave oven, which was another thing. When you're eating or cooking, you don't like to think about worms. (Well, maybe *you* do.) If you're microwaving some bacon, you can't help noticing that it's worm colored. When you've just stirred a vat of worms, you can't help worrying about what's in your lasagna. And forget about frying up a batch of onion rings and having one in your mouth when you happen to walk by the turtle tank and notice that Snappingy has a worm in *his* mouth.

But look what's happened! This chapter was supposed to be about Snappingy, and already the worms have taken over! See what I mean when I say I think about them too much? I suppose the worms would say they're just as interesting as any turtle, BUT WORMS CAN'T TALK, CAN THEY? So let's go back to our real topic—worms. I mean, *Snappingy*.

Like so many of my animals, Snappingy started out living at my friend Banjie's. Banjie's house is full of wonders. She has a night-blooming cereus—a huge plant that blooms only one night a year. She has a parrot named Shadow who loves to watch children's TV. Shadow has learned to sing the *Teletubbies* theme song, but she's made one change to the lyrics. Here's how Shadow's version goes:

> Over the hills and far away,
> Teletubbies come to play. . . .
> Time for teletubbies!
> Tinky Winky,
> Dipsy,
> Laa Laa,
> Po,
> Elmo . . .
> Teletubbies
> Say hello!

For anyone out there who doesn't know what TV is, I should tell you that Elmo lives on Sesame Street, not in Teletubbyland. In Shadow's opinion, though, Elmo belongs with the other four soft, plushy, high-voiced characters. Isn't that smart of her?

Anyway, one September morning Banjie's husband brought her eleven snapping-turtle eggs he had found near a pond. Neither Banjie nor Steve thought the eggs were still alive, or active, or whatever you call unhatched eggs. Banjie used them as a subject for a drawing or two, and then put them into a cup and left them on her attic stairs to store with her nature supplies another time. A few hours later, she had to go up to the attic for some reason. She was amazed to see that the cup now held eleven tiny baby turtles scrambling and jostling over one another in their efforts to get out of the cup. What if Banjie hadn't come back into the attic in time to find them? But luckily she did, and she put them into a tank of shallow water to keep for a few days.

"Want one?" asked Banjie when I was at her house marveling over the babies. They looked as if they were made of black rubber, and they were about the size of a bottle cap.

"Sure!" I said. No one had ever offered me a snapping turtle before.

"Take two," Banjie went on. "They're small."

So home I went home with my new babies.

I wasn't planning to keep the turtles. It was still nice and warm out, and I knew they'd need plenty of time to dig under the mud and begin their hibernation before the weather cooled off. Newly hatched snappers come out of their eggs in the fall and don't do much except find a nice place to hibernate. Their lives won't really get going until the following spring, when they dig up from under the mud and start looking for food. So I thought I'd hang on to the turtles for a couple of days and then let them go by the pond where Steve had found the eggs.

After a couple of days, though, my resolve began to ooze away, and I started in on my usual list of Reasons Why I Should Get to Keep Whatever Animal It Is. What if I let only one of the babies go and held on to the other throughout the winter? That way, I'd get to do so many fun things:

- I'd get to "study" a snapping turtle up close. Which would help snapping turtles in general, because now they'd have one more friend who "understands" them.

- I'd know that maybe I was increasing the odds of the "kept" turtle's surviving. Most baby snappers are so bite sized that they're eaten by predators within a few days of hatching. If I could release a turtle in the springtime, after it had grown a bit, it would be bigger and stronger and less likely to be caught by a heron, a raccoon, or whatever else eats baby turtles. Or at least this was what I told myself.

- I'd feel less guilty about keeping one turtle (well, borrowing it from the wild for a few months) because I'd know I had released the other one.

- I'd be able to use an aquarium I already owned and not have to buy a new one. Snapping turtles can live for fifty years and reach weights of up to seventy pounds. That would require a *huge* tank, obviously. (Plus, there would be the biting-fingers-off thing.) But I could keep my tiny turtle in a regular twenty-gallon tank, which wouldn't be too hard to clean.

I did such a good job with my reasoning that, before long, I was patting myself on the back for having decided to let Snappingy spend *only* the winter with us. What if I'd been greedy and decided to keep him all his life, the way some people do? How selfish that would have been, and what a lot of work for me if I'd reached the age of a hundred and still been taking care of a huge turtle! Keeping him for the winter was really the most *sensible* thing I could do.

Filled with virtue, I took Snappingy's twin to the pond and let him go in the grass. Instantly, he began scrambling toward the pond, burrowing under the grass as he went. In a couple of seconds he was out of sight, and I returned home to get Snappingy set up for a winter visit at our house.

Reptiles have a lot of needs. They need the right temperature and the right kind of light, or they get all kinds of infections. If they're aquatic, like Snappingy, they need very, very clean water to live in; otherwise, it would be like living in a toilet. By the time I was done setting up Snappingy's tank, he was surrounded by technology. He had a heater in his tank to keep the water at eighty-two degrees, and a filter, and a ceramic reptile lamp to give him a second source of heat and some light to bask in. There were some rocks he could climb on or hide under. And then, somewhere in the tank, there was teeny little Snappingy.

"He wouldn't need all that stuff in the wild," my husband kept pointing out.

"I know, but he isn't *in* the wild!" I kept answering. "If he were in the wild, he'd be hibernating now! Since he's not going to hibernate, he *has* to have the right conditions!"

Luckily, Snappingy didn't need any food for the first month. Baby snappers hatch with a soft, gray, gross-looking egg sac on the bottom of their shells. (Imagine a regular egg yolk; now imagine that it's gray and spongy. There you go!) They get nutrition from the egg sac for the first weeks of their life. Being my usual self, though, I couldn't believe Snappingy could possibly survive without real food, so I kept dropping mealworms and dried shrimp into his tank. He never even seemed to see them.

Maybe he'd like vegetables more, I thought. I tried shreds of lettuce and sliced grapes. Snappingy ignored these, too. All they did was make his tank dirty.

And then one day I dropped in a mealworm—and Snappingy *snapped* at it!

He really did. His tiny jaws clamped with such force that he shot backward in the water. He missed, and tried again. That time he managed to clamp onto the mealworm. He was still so little that the mealworm wriggled out of his mouth—which was a pretty pink inside, I noticed—but it was a start.

By the end of that week, Snappingy was catching mealworms and shreds of chicken like a pro. He would maneuver a mealworm around with his beaky lips until it poked out of his mouth like a cigar. Then—chomp,

chomp, chomp—he would slowly gulp it down. Sometimes part of the worm came back up, and Snappingy would have to re-chomp it. (It won't do any of us any good to imagine what the worm was thinking at that point.) "You're such a big boy!" I cooed at him. "You know how to eat *and* smoke a cigar!"

Around then, I switched to red worms, since they're more nutritious and more like what Snappingy would find in the wild. After that, he grew amazingly fast. When we first got him, all anyone said was, "He's so *tiny!*" They never say that now. Snappingy has become pet-turtle-sized—about the size and thickness of a doorknob. He's so fat that his shell looks too small on him. That's typical of snapping turtles, but sometimes I can't help wondering if Snappingy may be a little *too* fat. His armpits and what you might call his "leg pits" bulge out as if he were the worst kind of weightlifter. His legs look more like elephant legs with bear claws than anything you'd normally expect to see on a reptile. I hope he's not eating because he's bored. But if he is, he has only a few months more of boredom at our house.

John and I have come to love Snappingy. (It's amazing how many expressions you think you see in a turtle's face. He can just be staring at nothing, and I'll think he's worried.) But David *really* loves him. He *always, always* tells me I'm making the water in Snappingy's tank too deep. "He can't breathe!" David will complain.

"He can, if he swims up to the surface or climbs on his rocks," I answer. "If you're so worried about his breathing, *you* can change his water and clean his filter."

"And that's another thing," David goes on. "Those rocks. They're not arranged right."

"Snappingy doesn't care how they're arranged!"

"He needs a cozy bed," David insists, "and I'm going to make him one." Then he reaches into the tank with a fishnet and pushes the rocks into a corner of the tank.

"They don't look cozy to me," I grumble. "They're still just rocks."

But David always tells me I'm lucky to be married to someone who cares enough to make a nice bed for a turtle.

"I wonder what Snappingy is thinking," David once said dreamily.

I suspect that turtles don't do a ton of thinking, but Snappingy does know who we are. I don't mean he knows us individually, but he has realized that we're the ones who feed him. When he's hungry, he comes up to the front of his tank and stares, stares, *stares* at us. If he had any expressions, you'd say he had a "commanding" expression in his round eyes.

I drop in a worm, and it lands behind him. For a few seconds he doesn't realize it's there, and keeps trying to hypnotize me with his gaze. Then, suddenly, he sees the worm twisting around behind him and rushes for it. But I said I wouldn't talk about worms anymore, didn't I?

No matter how fat he may become, there's no need to worry that Snappingy will get too used to being fed by us. Once he's back in the wild, his hunting instincts will take over. He's sometimes picky with us, though. It seems that he actually gets sick of eating the same thing for too long. At least, he'll sometimes give me his "food stare" and then ignore whatever I drop in. Then I feed him something else—a little shrimp or a shred of roast beef. I don't see any reason not to spoil him while he's here. He'll never get spoiled by cruel, cruel nature.

Which reminds me: I've done a lot of reading about snapping turtles, and I'm sick of hearing people say they're "vicious." Vicious means "mean on purpose," and snappers can't *help* the way they snap at food. That's how they catch stuff! Their tongue is fixed inside their mouths so that it doesn't move. They don't have any teeth, just a "beak" on their upper jaw. Snapping replaces biting and chewing for them.

And yes, a big snapping turtle will snap at someone's hand—or at a stick you poke at him—but what else is he supposed to do? What other weapons does he have? Snappers can't retract their heads or legs into their shells the way other turtles can. It's not vicious to try to stop a person from bothering you.

I'm not saying you should do what my friend Tim did when he was a boy. That is, you should not pick up a huge snapping turtle and carry him around in your bike basket to a vacant lot and have all your friends stand around in a circle looking at him. That would be dangerous and mean. Still, I hope Snappingy will bite my finger once before I release him. He's too little to do any damage, and I'd love to be able to say I'd been bitten by a snapping turtle.

Right now he doesn't even try to bite me when I give him a bath under the faucet. He just closes his eyes, squinches up his little face, and tries to puuuuuuuush my fingers away with his thick, squat legs. When I put him back into his tank, he steers himself into a corner and paddles madly, going nowhere. Then I drop in a superworm, and that calms him down.

Because I forgot to say: We all got so grossed out by Snappingy's red worms that recently I switched to another kind of live insect called a superworm. Superworms aren't much better than red worms. In fact, they may be worse. They look like mealworms—tan and scaly, with tiny scrabbling legs—but they're about the size of my little finger. And their scrabbling legs can grab on to your finger when you're trying to drop them into Snappingy's tank.

"Every time I come home for vacation, you're feeding Snappingy something worse than before!" Laura complained the last time she visited. But at least superworms don't live in dirt, and at least they don't keep having babies. And at least that one time I dropped their bin on the kitchen floor, all I had to do was sweep them up with a dustpan and brush. I didn't have to MOVE OUT OF THE HOUSE, the way I'd have had to do if they'd been red worms.

But I said I wasn't going to talk about worms anymore, didn't I?

goodbye to my barnyard?

What's next in my animal lineup?

I'm not sure.

I'm not even sure there's going to be a next.

Oh, I'll probably always have *some* animals around. The pets I have now are going to be around for several more years. I'm fifty-one years old. (If you've forgotten about that, go back and read the introduction.) By the time my last guinea pig dies, I'll probably be close to sixty.

And I'm sure that a stray cat or two will show up at my door one day, and I'll feed it, and things will go on from there.

And I've never adopted a dog from a shelter, and that's one of my goals at some point.

But . . . more birds? More hamsters? I wonder.

I haven't done much traveling. If I want to see the world, I'd like to do it without worrying about how well my pet sitter is doing back home.

And if I really want to work on my dollhouse miniatures—and I do!—that's as much a full-time activity as the pets are. I'm not sure I can do both.

And—let's be honest here—I sometimes get sick of cleaning cages. Especially when I realize I've been doing it for twenty years. Do I want to clean cages for *another* twenty?

My children say yes. "When I have kids, I want them to be able to visit your guinea pigs," Laura told me recently. Well, I'd like that, too.

My nieces and nephews and godchildren and the kids in my neighborhood would also prefer to keep visiting new animals at my house. Sometimes, a kid will ask me, "How many pets do you have now?" And he'll be disappointed with my answer. "Where are the hedgehogs?" he'll want to know. "What happened to Japan?"

But I can't keep getting new animals just for other people to visit.

So what I'm thinking is this: From here on in, maybe most of my animals will be visiting *me*.

Take Snappingy, for instance. We've loved having him here. He's been a great addition to our kitchen. But we'll love letting him go, too. It will be fun, in kind of a melancholy way, to release him at Emmons Pond, which is a huge expanse of water near our house. Maybe he'll bury himself right away. Maybe he'll take off into the water and swim far, far out, farther than he's ever been able to swim in his tank—and all we'll see will be the ripples as he disappears.

We'll miss him, but we'll know he's where he should be. And every time we drive or bike past Emmons Pond, we'll send him a hello, just the way I say hi to Pecky whenever I hear a screech owl.

And certainly whenever I hear a blue jay or a robin— or, most often, a starling—I wonder if I knew that bird as a baby.

I'm going to have more and more empty cages as time goes on. Why don't I use them to help rehabilitate wild animals so they can go back to their natural homes? What if one day I was lucky enough to help raise a baby crow? Or a fox kit? Or even a fawn?

Even just more starlings would be fine. My point is, from here on in I'm not sure I want to *own* more animals. If I can see them up close for a short time, that may be enough.

Years ago, before my husband and I moved to the country, we lived in New York City. One of my favorite times of year was spring. Well, duh. I guess that's *most* people's favorite time of year. What I should have said is one of my favorite things about the springtime was looking up at the lampposts. Unless you looked, you'd never know that in springtime in New York City, the top of every single lamppost has a nest of sparrows in it. After work I'd walk home checking each lamp. In early spring, the parent sparrows would be flying in and out with nesting materials. As the weeks went on, I'd see them bringing food to their babies. And by summer, the lampposts would be empty again.

I would look down at the sparrows bustling around on the sidewalks, bathing in puddles and pecking at horse manure from the carriage horses around Central Park. (There are always a few oats left in horse manure, and sparrows like to check it out.) Or they'd be standing shyly at the edge of a pigeon flock, waiting their turn for the popcorn someone had spilled. They didn't expect any of the whole pieces—those were for the pigeons. Once in a while, though, an especially brave sparrow would suddenly dart in among the bigger birds and grab a kernel for himself. Then he would fly away to eat it in private.

"Now, which nest did you hatch in?" I'd think. "Were you in the lamppost at the corner of Sixty-ninth Street and Second Avenue or the one in front of the wine store? And where will I see *your* babies?"

Here's my point: You don't have to own an animal to love it. And the more animals you *don't* own, the more of them you're free to love.

But then just today I read an ad about an abandoned rabbit who needs a home. She's missing an ear, so no one wants her. . . .

And it might be fun to put the nesting box back into the finches' cage. . . .

And my stock of pygmy mice is dwindling. . . .

What do *you* think I should do?